APA – AUSTRIA PRESS AGENCY
BANK AUSTRIA – UNICREDIT GROUP

•

JOURNEYS TO THE HEART OF EUROPE

APA – Austria Press Agency
Bank Austria – UniCredit Group

Which road to Europe

Contributions to the Journalism Prize
»Writing For CEE«

Edited
by
Ambros Kindel

Wieser *Verlag*

Wieser Verlag

A-9020 Klagenfurt/Celovec, Ebentaler Straße 34b
Telefon: +43(0)463 37036 Fax: +(0)463 37635
office@wieser-verlag.com
www.wieser-verlag.com

ISBN-978-3-85129-805-5

Table of Contents

Europe – an Exciting Project

This year we are proud to celebrate the 5th anniversary of the renowned journalism award »Writing for Central and Eastern Europe«. Five years of good cooperation between Bank Austria and the Austrian Press Agency (APA), five years of critical discussion on European integration by journalists all over Europe. This prize has been promoting European integration for several years now by presenting critical and constructive journalism that can help eliminate barriers and prejudices, and facilitate a positive discussion of Europe's future. With this publication we therefore offer a selection of journalistic contributions to show the different attitudes of journalists to the topic »Europe«.

Europe is an exciting project. But what has happened in the last five years? Many European countries have joined the European Union, a number of nations have adopted the euro as their currency, and many of them are living the spirit of a common Union. But there are still some questions that need to be answered: Ireland's »no« to the Treaty of Lisbon, the integration of Turkey into the European Union, and the political challenges in Russia. These topics are important in politics and journalism as never before, where the media has a central and special role.

Bank Austria, as a member of UniCredit Group, has far-reaching experience in Central and Eastern Europe, not only in business with currently 28 million customers and more than 83,000 employees, but also in other sectors. The bank has been supporting numerous young authors, artists and musicians in the region for many years and sees this commitment as a reflection of the long, successful relationship between Austria and CEE. UniCredit Group itself has strong ties with the CEE region and operates the largest network there.

I do hope that you will enjoy reading this collection of excellent and exciting articles we have put together from the best articles every year.

Erich Hampel
Chairman Austria & CEE Region, UniCredit Group
CEO, Bank Austria

Writing for CEE

The motto of the journalism prize awarded annually by the Austrian Press Agency and Bank Austria (Member of UniCredit Group) is programmatic for the journalistic work of the Austrian news agency. We cover not only Austrian, European and international events in the areas of politics, economy, history, culture and sport, but we have also been focusing on countries in Central and Eastern Europe and Southeast Europe for years.

A network of correspondents was built in the course of the early nineties, covering the Czech Republic, Slovakia, Hungary, Slovenia, Croatia and Serbia. Later this network was extended to include Poland, Bulgaria, Romania, Scandinavia and the Baltic nations of Lithuania, Estonia and Latvia.

In doing this, the APA developed its very own approach. We do not send staff to these countries and – with the exception of the EU office in Brussels – we do not maintain correspondents' offices either. We hire qualified journalists from the CEE countries who cover their own countries for the APA comprehensively and authentically.

In the Vienna headquarters, we have colleagues who specialise in these countries and speak their languages. Our APA team includes colleagues who are able to work in Czech, Slovakian, Hungarian, Slovene, Croatian, Serbian, Polish and Russian.

The journalist award »Writing for CEE« is, in a way, the continuation of the APA's years of endeavours towards coverage from this area. The annual award forms a harmonious whole with an important part of our daily work. The APA sees itself – also – as a CEE agency.

Journalists from the countries of Central and Southeast Europe will be invited to compete for the »Writing for CEE« award in the future, too. The goal of the award is to encourage the journalistic discussion of questions regarding European integration. According to the organisers, journalists from non-EU countries such as the Ukraine, Belarus or Russia are also invited to participate. The prize winner receives 5000 euros.

The collection of editorial works presented in this book is a demonstration of a highly topical and profound journalism which impresses us and starts us thinking.

Enjoy yourself reading.

Michael Lang
Editor in Chief
APA – Austria Press Agency

The Improvement of Central Europe

The Best of Five Years of the Writing for CEE Journalism Prize

Ambros Kindel

Austrian literature enfant terrible Oswald Wiener wrote an anti-novel in the 1960's entitled *The Improvement of Central Europe*. At a time of East-West confrontation bristling with weapons, barely-peaceful coexistence, the Cold War and the Iron Curtain through Europe, even talk about »improving« Central Europe had a sarcastic aura of surrealism.

Today, too, we must beware of a euphoric view of Europe. The continent does not only rest on outstanding achievements in all areas of the human spirit. True, Europe is founded on a grand synthesis of Christian revelation and analytic Greek philosophy; of course, it rests on the values of democracy, individualism and human rights. But it also stands on ruins: the mass graves of victims of brutal massacres and inconceivable crimes....

Now, twenty years after the fall of the Iron Curtain, the countries of Central Europe know very little about each other. The reports in the media concentrate on abbreviated news about politics and economics. There are too few explanatory background stories about developments in the neighbouring countries -

and about the fears and concerns of the people living there.

Neighbours should not remain unknown to each other. They must inform themselves about each other, and they must know about each other. Each of the neighbours in Central Europe must have a picture of the others. The media must transmit this picture in detail, and without distortions.

If we want to be informed about our neighbours, we need detailed reporting about their political, economic, social and cultural development. We need more details and more continuity than is provided by the international news agencies and media which give the big headlines and then turn elsewhere.

These are the reasons why the Austria Press Agency and Bank Austria launched the Writing for CEE journalism prize in 2004, the year of the biggest enlargement in EU history. Let me give a brief overview of the journalistic contributions selected for this booklet.

Faces of Europe - in the Refugee Camps

In 2008, radio journalist Anna Koktsidou, who was born in Greece and works in Germany, was awarded the Writing for CEE prize for her reports about migrants and asylum-seekers in South East Europe. For weeks she travelled through the Balkans to see camps and talk with people in them from South East Europe and all parts of the world.

From Anna Koktsidou's research emerged a Deutschlandfunk report of particular intensity and with an unusual amount of facts. It was a report which made it again clear to us how wrong it is to confront people forced to leave their home countries with populist slogans.

Scar Tissue from the Iron Curtain

»The World Behind Vienna«: Austrian author and journalist Martin Leidenfrost received the 2007 prize for a cycle of literary-style reports. Leidenfrost presented journalistic excursions through a region often named Central Europe and occasionally Centrope, which glitters with its cultural diversity, but still means little more to some Austrians than »former Eastern Bloc«.

Martin Leidenfrost has been living in the Slovak border village of Devinska Nova Ves for three years. He describes it as slowly-healing scar tissue from the Iron Curtain. »I'm an Austrian, and have one kilometer to go to Austria, 30 kilometers to Hungary, and 50 to the Czech Republic. From this perspective, the region appears as one of natural unity. It's the vantage point from which I write.«

Editorial Office Six Metres Underground

The article by the Bosnian journalist Šefik Dautbegovic, who received the Writing for CEE award in 2006, describes the voyage of his torn country to Europe. Dautbegovic criticizes his country in an ironic way and also satirically. He criticizes his country as only a patriot would. Even if a Bosnian patriot has already overcome the division, partition and disruption of his country....

Šefik Dautbegovic is a journalist working for the daily newspaper Oslobodjenje, published in Sarajevo. He also spent the years of the Bosnian War (1992-95) there. His editorial office was in a cellar six metres underground. Dautbegovic wrote his articles for Oslobodjenje on an old typewriter. Candles were his only source of light.

Mrs. Bulgarian

In 2005, Bulgarian journalist Diana Ivanova received the award. Born in Montana, Bulgaria, in 1968, she spent one year of studies in Vienna. Her astonishment at the fact that many Viennese frankly admit that they have never visited the neighbouring city of Bratislava dates back to that time.

One of the texts from the prizewinning series »Hello Melancholy« is about a woman from Bulgaria who lives in Vienna, a waitress who seems to have no name but is called simply »Mrs. Bulgarian« by everyone. People who come to the West from the East of Europe not only lose their names, writes the prize winner, but any right to nostalgia as well. In their post-Communist home country there just isn't enough one might remember nostalgically. What remains is melancholy....

In her work, Diana Ivanova depicts sensitive images of humanity. It is a subjective view of the world between the East and the West. At the presentation of the award in November 2005, she convinced the audience not only by the quality of her journalistic work, but also by her theoretical reflections. Her remark that the subjective view of mankind was the focus of her attention because Marxism-Leninism had abused objectivity to »obliterate individuality« won spontaneous applause.

The Seventh Lack of Power

The year before, Luboš Palata, head of the foreign affairs department of the Prague newspaper Lidové Noviny, had received our journalism prize. »The idea was simply quite absurd to me that someone would want to kill me just because I wrote a few lines about him in the paper«: Palata quotes the Czech journalist Sabina Slonkova, who nearly fell victim to a murder attempt in 2002. A high-ranking former diplomat engaged a criminal to murder the journalist who had written unwelcome articles about him. Sabina Slonkova survived because the would-be murderer, who had already taken the money for his commission, went to the police.

Reflecting on Sabina Slonkova's amazement at her narrow escape, Palata analyzes the situation of journalists in the reform states in his article »The Seventh Lack of Power«, »For members of the Mafia we are nothing, and today the communists laugh about us. «. The privatizers were often profiteers who had made their pile for generations to come. And the politicians despised journalists as »irritating vermin«. Palata's pessimistic conclusion: Journalists should supervise those in power - they should be the seventh power, but are only »The Seventh Lack of Power«.

After the Fall of the Iron Curtain

To reach our conclusion: Sometimes when we Austrians say »Central Europe«, our neighbours hear »Habsburg Empire«. Let me emphasize that the idea of Writing for CEE is absolutely free from such outdated nostalgia. This is guaranteed by the members of the jury* whose spokesman I have the honour to be. And this is guaranteed by the contributions to the Writing for CEE journalism prize, which I present in this book.

Let us remember. In 1989 the walls and dictatorships fell. The Iron Curtain fell, and for the first time in ages, we stood face to face with our neighbours without coercion. The barbed wire was cut, rifts were covered. Socialist reality had ceased to exist. The doors were open and the way ahead appeared free. Promptly, in the West, fear arose of the new freedom. Once more, one sees that history does not go in straight lines, but may sometimes swing like a pendulum.

Neighbours need not love each other, they do not even have to like each other. But they should always be ready for dialogue and cooperation, above all when they want to push through joint interests in the future Europe. They should work together in processing painful history in order to get to a joint view of past events.

We neighbours should inform each other authentically and with our own efforts. If we are talking about good neighbourliness in central Europe today, we are talking about a truly historic opportunity. Europe appears genuinely about to learn the lessons of past horrors, and make the way to peace and cooperation irreversible. And Central Europe is always at the centre of events.

The partition of Europe has been overcome. Reunification of the continent has started. »Improving« Central Europe is no longer a satire. The improvement of Central Europe has really been underway - since 1989.

The contributions compiled in this publication offer a reflective and a realistic picture of Europe. A journalism prize should not serve as an embellishment, but an incentive to outline and reflect on topics and problems. This contemplation can be highly rewarding, especially if it has been written in such an outstanding journalistic and linguistic form as the present contributions.

***Ambros Kindel**, born 1954 in Vienna, journalist, Head of Foreign Department,* APA - Austria Press Agency, *Jury Speaker of* »Writing for CEE«, *Lecturer at Danube University, Krems, and at Austrian Institute for Training of Journalists (KfJ), Salzburg.*

* Over the past five years the following have been members of the jury:

Milan Berko, journalist, Bratislava
Samuel Brečka, Comenius University, Bratislava
Zbynek Fiala, journalist and media consultant, Prague
Grzegorz Gauden, publisher and publicist , Warsaw
Jože Hudeček, author, Ljubljana
Ildiko Füredi-Kolarik, spokesperson, Vienna
Igor Janke, journalist, Warsaw
Pawel Lisicki, journalist, Warsaw
Jiří Pehe, New York University, Prague
Milan Smid, Charles University, Prague
Júlia Váradi, journalist, Budapest
Ambros Kindel, journalist, Vienna

Die Furche Weekly Magazine, Austria, 8 June 2006

The Centre is in the East (2006)

About 80 communities claim to be at the centre of Europe. Wolfgang Bahr has been to three of them.

By Wolfgang Bahr

It is amazing how many states, regions and municipalities use the term »centre« for their websites. www.poland.gov.pl, for example, states in its »Facts« file that »Poland lies in the central part of the European continent, the geometric centre of which is near Warsaw.« A certain naïvité is evident in the claims made by Potsdam, and its Lord Mayor's bland assertion that »it just so happens that our city is geographically in the middle of the continent«; on the other hand, the more combative Piedmont informs us that it »has chosen to play an increasingly central role in the European Union – and that means geographically too.« Centrality has been claimed for places as far apart as Northern Ireland and the Székely region of Rumania.

In view of all this, Austria now puts surprisingly little emphasis on its position at the heart of Europe. Even during its EU presidency, rhetorical exploitation of the country's geopolitical location was remarkably restrained; apparently being at the centre has become so natural that it no longer needs to be stressed. This is markedly different from the period just after World War II, when Austria's national anthem stressed the country's »strong heart,« in the wake of an episode when this heart had stopped beating completely for some years. Today the federal capital has been emboldened to plan a railway station that was originally to be called »Vienna – Centre of Europe«, and to devise for itself a leading role in a region named Centrope, together with the cities of Bratislava, Brno and Győr. Apart from Vienna, a specific Austrian tradition of claiming to be at the centre seems to have survived only in Braunau, apparently based on a statement made by Napoleon. But there again, Waldsassen in Bavaria likewise calls upon the Corsican's geopolitical point of view to help make a similar claim....

Bernotai, Lithuania

Much more solidly based are the claims of Lithuania, which has defeated all its competitors in the struggle to claim Europe's geographical middle point. They rest on calculations made by the National Geographical Institute in Paris, which in 1989 detected the centre of Europe 26 kilometres north of Vilnius. First the Lithuanian independence movement, and then the tourist industry, picked up on the annoyance factor of fixing the centre so far to the East and used it to generate publicity. But it was an artist's private enterprise that first made the theory of Lithuanian centrality a live issue.

»Europos Centras« at Purnuškäs, more precisely at nearby Bernotai, celebrates Lithuania's accession to the European Union – and also to NATO, albeit in a somewhat obscure manner, by means of a compass dug into the ground. The republic has invested quite a substantial sum in building a festival square displaying the flags of the EU member states and a granite column with a gilded wreath of stars. A friendly clerk supplies you with a visitor's certificate. A golf course is currently under construction in the monument's well-cared for grounds.

The »Europos Parkas«, several kilometres away, is quite different, an imposing open-air museum of contemporary art and one of Lithuania's main tourist attractions. Its creator, 38-year old Gintaras Karosas, has not only succeeded in persuading world-renowned artists, such as Dennis Oppenheim and Sol LeWitt, to supply designs, but has also got sponsorship for realization of the objects, some of which are of colossal dimensions. His own Monument of the Centre of Europe is comparatively restrained: stone slabs indicating the distances to all the European capitals are arranged on the lawn, forming a vast circle around a pyramid.

Cognoscenti of historical ironies will note that Minsk is portrayed as the closest city in geographical terms – and the most distant in terms of ideology.

For artist and landscape designer Karosas, whose grandfather was forced to emigrate, and whose father was deported to Siberia at the age of 14, Europe is an affair of the heart, but more importantly a symbol of creativity and a challenge to the individual. In the vast park, a balance is struck between nature and art, likewise between the individual, nationalism and the community of nations: »Nationalism, when it takes the form of regarding oneself as better than everybody else, is absurd, but a clearly defined national identity is a progressive influence on those who share it.«

Kremnické Bane, Slovakia

While Gintaras Karosas is acidly critical of an administration perpetuating the mannerisms, if not the methods, of the ancien régime, and of careerists addicted to fashionable neo-liberalism, Ján Priwitzer, the mayor of Kremnické Bane in central Slovakia, is even more disillusioned. When Vladimír MeĐiar led his country towards independence, a great future seemed to emerge for the village. A memorial stone was erected close to the old church of Saint John which, according to legend, had been built on the present site at the command of angels in order to be »closer to the centre«. Like the column in Lithuania, it stresses national identity. A platform was built of natural stone, from which a »Message from the Centre of Europe« is proclaimed annually by the Matica Slovenská cultural organization. On May 1st, 2004, ten lime trees were planted on a nearby hill, one for every state joining the European Union on that day.

But the foundation stone for a Park of Slovak Emigration is still lying in the mayor's office and no funds have been raised so far for improving the infrastructure – there is only a modest Hotel Stred Evropy in nearby Krahule. Oddly enough, it seems to have been the change of government, to one led by Europhile Mikuláš Dzurinda, that has caused the project to be put on ice. At the same time, the Catholic authorities show little interest in the construction of a masonic »Temple of Europe«, whose presumed site is marked by a white stone. On the other hand, a Capuchin monastery was actually built near the church in the 1990s, with Austrian support.

In conversation, the open-minded Father Guardian traces the stormy course of Slovakian history, from the Tartar invasions to entry into the EU, and offers a rather prosaic explanation for the centre of Europe being sited here: apparently it is all down to Italian land surveyors, who had come to the »Slovakian Semmering« to build the local railway. He also stresses the area's traditionally peaceful cohabitation of Germans and Slovaks – to this day German hymns are sung at Sunday service, and Mayor Priwitzer, himself one of the last surviving ethnic Germans, serves as sacristan.

Havlíčkův Brod, Bohemia

There is also a German past in Havlíčkův Brod in Bohemia. This year the former Deutsch Brod commemorates the 150th anniversary of the death of Karel Havlíček-Borovský, the founder of Czech journalism, who was to lend his name to the city after World War II. The flat overlooking the Town Square, from which he was deported to Brixen one night by Austrian police, can still be seen, and Havlíček's »Tyrolean Elegies« are still part of the Czech literary canon.

There are indeed literary indications of such a provincial centre of Europe, and the city's spokeswoman remarks that a »sense of humour« is inseparable from local geopolitical ambitions. Since it proved difficult to find evidence of an earlier tradition of Brod as the centre of Europe, recourse was made to »the last remaining instance, the legacy of Jára Cimrman«. In Prague's Cimrman Theatre, the executors of this fictitious poet's fictive legacy confirmed that such a place was to be found »near Brod«. As Brod means »ford«, the search continued along the banks of the River Sázava and there, wonder of wonders, a glass ball was found....

The ball was incorporated into a wooden maquette and is now kept by the mayor to be displayed on special occasions. However there is free access to a monument in the middle of a small maze near the coffee house called At the Notary; it consists of a huge funnel through which occasional rain water may flow towards the alleged centre of Europe. A rolling ball, a maze, a funnel: these are symbols of a Europe that can hardly be forced into sterile geographical co-ordinates. According to the title of a sculpture in the Europos Parkas by Magdalena Abakanowicz, the continent should rather be seen as a »space of unknown growth«.

Wolfgang Bahr, *born Vienna-Mödling, 1950. Journalist, writer, and translator, concentrating on Central European and church affairs. Studied Austrian History and German Language at Vienna University, Doctor of Philosophy 1978. Contributor to periodicals including Die Furche, Kirche In, Österreichische Osthefte, Kathpress. Austrian Catholic News Agency co-worker. Editor-in-Chief, Memo – Ecumenical Manuscript Service of Religious Broadcasts on ORF Radio, 2000 to 2005. Books: Graz – Our Town, God in the Alps, Travels of the Dead. Presently researching Josef Hlávka for the Middle Class in the Hapsburg Monarchy project group, Institute of Economic and Social History, Vienna University.*

Welt am Sonntag, Germany, 7 May 2006

Departure Germany, Arrival Europe (2006)

By Antonia Beckermann

The day after tomorrow the European Union is celebrating its annual Europe Day; however, not many people know even in theory what this day is really about. Though in practice the European Community is quite alive – last but not least thanks to the low-cost carriers. How they promote the European identity can be gauged during a round trip: Five flights, five countries, 7,346 kilometres in three days for less than 300 euros.

Yesterday Berlin, today Tallinn, tomorrow Helsinki – altogether for 90 euros. Initially, Christiane Schreireis was planning to fly directly from Stuttgart to Finland. The 26-year old student wants to start her internship at the institute for molecular genetics in Helsinki. For this flight to Finland she would have had to pay double as much as she is now paying for all the three flights. »I would have had to do the internship at home, the direct flight was too expensive«, says Christiane.

Thanks to the low-cost carrier EasyJet, she was able to sit in the beer garden in Berlin yesterday, and visit the cathedral of Tallinn today; she will be working in the lab in Helsinki tomorrow. Three countries, three cultures in three days for a ridiculous price and without passport or customs control. Only Europe provides such an opportunity for its people. Most of the Europeans do not notice the impact of the European Union in their daily lives. By flying they are crossing borders both geographically and in their minds, and are automatically getting closer to each other.

By offering their services, Ryanair, EasyJet and the others have revolutionised the life of the Europeans. In a very short time they have succeeded in something politicians and diplomats have been working for for years: a European feeling of community.

Flight EZY 4605 from Berlin to Tallinn

»Don't ever use the toilet« is the first thing Nathaniel says. »As soon as you go, you've lost« – lost your sleeping space. The 24-year old from Chicago spent the night at the Berlin-Schoenefeld airport. With hundreds of others, the student has been scrambling for the few chairs and a few hours of sleep.

Nathaniel is on a trip through Europe: Madrid, Berlin, Tallinn, Helsinki, Rome and the Canary Islands. Europe in four weeks, all with low-cost carriers. »I wouldn't have come without the opportunity of such cheap flights. For us Americans this is special. You pay 20 euros and you can fly from one country to another.«

Germanwings, HLX and EasyJet: There are about 50 low-cost carriers in Europe. In 2005 they carried 135 million passengers. And the market is still growing. »Over the last few years our annual growth rate was between 20 and 25 percent«, says Roland Keppler, chairman of HLX. And there seems to be no end to the boom. In the coming years, experts expect growth rates of around 20 percent. They are certain: Without low-cost carriers, the mobility of the Europeans could not have developed so fast. One could even say that the European identity wouldn't have developed.

Nathaniel is one his way to Tallinn, the capital of Estonia. EasyJet was one of the first low-cost carriers to offer flights to the Baltic states, which joined the EU in 2004. The flight is fully booked. One of the passengers is Robert Busching. The 23-year old student from Berlin is flying to a Dianne Reeves concert. The jazz singer is also singing in Berlin. But for Robert it is cheaper to fly to Tallinn and go to the concert than to buy a concert ticket for Berlin. »70 euros would have been the ticket price for Berlin. Now I'm paying the same price for Tallinn and the concert.« Opinion polls show that 60 percent of the passengers wouldn't have made the trip without the cheap fare.

Eastern Europe is a growth market for low-cost carriers. More and more Western Europeans want to get to know their »new« neighbours. Former Royal Air Force pilot David Ledward came to Tallinn in 2004 to spend a weekend with friends. »I was curious. In the military I wasn't allowed to fly that far east,« he says. The Brit liked the city with its Hanseatic style so much that he came back again and again – twelve times altogether. On this trip he is finally buying a flat in Tallinn. In terms of flight passengers Estonia is – after Slovakia – the country where the air traffic has grown most.

Even the locals use the airplane more often. Marju Henre is one of them. How often she has been waiting for her plane to depart from Tallinn she cannot count. But it has been very often. The 27-year old Estonian spent parts of her studies in Great Britain. Thanks to the cheap flights, she can visit her family and friends more often.

Hundreds are waiting for their departure at London Stansted Airport. They are sitting on plastic chairs, on suitcases, on the floor: soccer fans following their team through Europe, couples on a short trip, retirees using their free time to see Europe. Nowhere else is the EU is so noticeable and alive. By looking for the right counter people overcome their language problems. Waiting for the security checks, British tourists and Spanish businesspeople exchange city tips. At the airport everyone strives for a common language.

Flight FR 9808 from London to Barcelona

The most popular flights in Europe are between Great Britain and Spain. Most of the passengers are tourists. One can notice it because their t-shirts and sun glasses do not fit the cloudy London weather. But also many companies use the low-cost carriers. Two or three times a month, Karl Richards flies to Spain. The 32-year old worksin the film business and spends a lot of time on airplanes. Even more so since the introduction of the cheap offers. Like many British people, he doesn't think very highly of the EU: »Europe doesn't give me anything, apart from a quicker check-in.«

Few people really connect their freedom of travel to the EU. Most of the passengers don't even know what the EU does, not to mention that it is the Schengen Agreement that made easy travel possible. Most travelers, especially the older ones, still have the feeling for borders. »In the past we had to stop with our car at each border. Today we just drive through«, remembers Monika Weiss. She and her husband have a flat in Barcelona. For 30 years they drove to Spain. For a couple of years they have been flying because it is faster and cheaper.

Flight FR 6901 from Barcelona to Brussels

Daniela Mojos and Humberto Carmona sport healthy tans. They are sitting at the Girona Airport waiting for their departure to Brussels. The two Chileans are on honeymoon. Daniela's sister told her about the cheap flights in Europe. »All four flights together are cheaper than one flight to Chile«, says the 30-year-old. Less tanned are the businesspeople with ties and briefcases that are sitting in the same hall. They work in Brussels or Barcelona, they live in Frankfurt or London. No problem with low-cost carriers.

In addition to other businesspeople, many lobbyists fly to the »capital of Europe«. A bus brings them directly from the airport to the Place Schumann in the European Quarter in Brussels. The day after tomorrow, Europe Day, people will remember one of the founding fathers of the EU. On the 9th of May, 1950, Robert Schumann, the former French foreign minister, first presented his idea of a common Europe. Today, around the Place Schumann, the European Commission and the European Council of Ministers have their offices. This is the place where the European Union is filled with substance, this is where the heart of the EU beats.

In the modern airport in Brussels, passengers are waiting for their Virgin Express flight to Berlin. The plane is delayed three hours. One of the passengers is Carl Wagner. The 55-year-old German works for the Technischer Überwachungs-Verein (Technical Monitoring Association). Every two weeks he flies through Europe, mainly to Belgium, Great Britain and Scandinavia. »Thanks to the low-cost carriers, it is easier to service a client in London or Madrid than to drive 200 kilometres in Germany.«

Many companies use the cheap air connections to open local branches in other European countries. »The number of business trips has grown by 30 percent«, says Christoph Burmann, who is researching the impact of the low-cost carriers at Bremen University.

Spanish businesspeople, German tourists, Estonian students: the low-cost carriers attract all people and nationalities. For little money, everyone has the opportunity to get to know their neighbouring countries and people. This brings the EU together more than any European regulation and it is more important than the little-known Europe Day. The Europeans want to use their freedom, in business and privately. Thanks to the low-cost carriers they can do just that. Plentifully and without borders.

***Antonia Beckermann**, born 1979 in Frankfurt am Main, Germany. Since 2005 junior editor, politics department, Welt am Sonntag, Axel-Springer journalism school. 2003–2004 freelancer for the Second German Television (ZDF) editorial department for foreign policy. 2000–2001 freelancer for the Neue Osnabruecker Zeitung. Education: Master of Arts in Contemporary European Studies at the University of Bath, Great Britain; Bachelor of Arts in European Studies at the University of Osnabrueck, Germany.*

Pittsburgh Tribune-Review, USA, 12 September 2003

Genealogy Quest Leads Reporter to Rural Slovakia (2004)

By Andrew Conte

CHMINIANSKE JAKUBOVANY, Slovakia – No one here knows my great-grandfather. He left this rural village of family farm plots 100 years ago without looking back.

Now, three generations later, my inquiries about his life draw bemused looks and a curious reception. One family with the same last name even posed for photos, though protesting they could be no more than distant cousins.

Retracing the footsteps of Andre Sedlak, these tenuous links have been enough.

In a nation of immigrants, genealogy has become a popular American pastime with families seeking to retell their stories. The search, like mine, can be complicated by a lack of records, language barriers, distance and the passage of time.

With the Internet, local guides and more than a little luck, my mother, Olive Marie (Sedlak) Conte, and I completed our ancestral journey this summer.

While unique to me, my great-grandfather's story has been repeated a million times or more.

So many Slovaks made similar trips at the last turn of the century that it seems everyone here has a relative who came to Pittsburgh. More Slovaks settled in Pennsylvania than any other state, and 50,000 of the immigrants and their descendents live in Allegheny County today.

Cultural ties between the city and Slovakia remain obvious. Dozens of Slovak social clubs are maintained throughout the region. Just last year, Pittsburgh adopted Slovakia's third-largest city, Presov, as its newest »sister city.«

»The perception of people is that Pittsburgh is the capital of the ›second Slovakia‹,« says Milan Benc, mayor of Presov, whose cousin lives in Derry, Pennsylvania.

But while public bonds are strong, personal ones can be fragile.

My journey here started with Andre Sedlak's baptismal certificate, a few black-and-white photos of him in America and bits of family history recalled by my mother, her aunts and uncles and cousins.

Written in Hungarian with archaic place names, the baptismal record offered a start but only that. The University of Pittsburgh's Slavic Language Department gave me the name of a professor's wife, Emily Swan, who translated the certificate into English.

That revealed my great-great-grandparents' names, their village, their street address and information about their church. Lutherans in a predominantly Roman Catholic country, they were a religious minority but lived in an enclave of other Protestants.

My excitement was immediately dampened by the realization that the village name, Jakabvagasa, was Hungarian and no longer exists.

Thanks to the Internet, that was not as insurmountable as it first seemed. A Web site called »East Slovakia Genealogy Research Strategies« (www.iabsi.com/gen/public) offered some of the best advice for starting out.

Online assistance

Peter Nagy, a Slovak who runs his own Internet site (www.centroconsult.sk) and genealogical research service, looks up historic place names for free. He responded to an e-mail inquiry overnight, giving me the modern village name of »Chminianske Jakubovany.«

I easily located the village online at MapQuest (www.mapquest.com), finding it about 10 miles west of Presov.

As in my own family, many Slovaks stayed in America but many others did not.

When Sedlak and his three brothers left their village, two of them immediately returned and the other two never looked back. My great-grandfather settled in the Monongahela Valley, and his brother ventured on to Ohio.

Slovaks who came back from America often had saved up enough money working in mines and mills to afford their own small plot of land. Then, when the Socialists took over the country through World War II, thousands lost their homesteads and their savings.

»My grandfather went to Pittsburgh to work in the mines and came back,« says Imrich Fulop, deputy director of the Kosice Self-Governing Region, Eastern Slovakia's largest state. »The only difference between those who stayed and those who returned is that we're still poor.«

Unemployment in some rural villages here tops 80 percent today, but many of the small family farms have been restored.

Arriving here, we stopped at the first farm house with people outside. With the help of a guide, we asked whether they knew any Sedlaks in the village, and they did. In Slovak, my family name means »farmer« or »villager,« something akin to Smith or Jones in the United States.

The patriarch of the family hopped in our car and led us to a house owned by a man named George Sedlak, the same name as one of Andre's brothers but too young to be of the same generation.

Sedlak, 82, said his father had the same name but did not have any brothers in America. At best, then, we were no more than distant cousins. But because they looked like my American relatives and because they were so gracious, my mother and I posed for a couple of pictures.

Eager for any other contact, we sought out the Lutheran church where Andre Sedlak had been baptized. The village minister, who lives in the church with his wife and son, led us into his office.

Our baptismal certificate gives specific details about church records, but the book containing them no longer exists. More recent records, dating to the early 19th century, showed that Andre Sedlak's brother, George, had at least one child who died shortly after birth. No other details were available.

Then the minister led us into the sanctuary, the spiritual climax of our journey.

In a room that had been added midway through the 20th century, wooden pews sat in rows below crystal chandeliers and an ornate painted ceiling.

Passing through an archway emblazoned in brown paint with Slovak scripture, we found the white-marble font where my great-grandfather had been baptized 135 years earlier.

After months of research, I had at last found a connection across the generations to my great-grandfather, who had died even before my mother was born. In that moment, we reconnected the century-old circle of my family's story.

***Andrew Conte**, born 1971, newspaper journalist based in Pittsburgh, Pennsylvania. Reported from Russia before the collapse of communism. Works now as an freelance reporter for the Pittsburgh Tribune-Review, covering a broad range of investigative topics. Graduated with a master's degree from Columbia University's School of Journalism in 1997. Won numerous journalism awards and was named the Pittsburgh Tribune-Review's reporter of the year in 2004. Conte teaches journalism at the University of Pittsburgh. He lives outside Pittsburgh with his wife, Tania, and their two children, Noah and Claudia.*

Oslobodjenje Newspaper, Bosnia-Herzegovina, June 2006

My country – Which Road to Europe
(2006 winner)

We are headed toward the place where normal people went long ago

By Šefik Dautbegovic

The bogey about Bosnia no longer wanders around Europe, which has opened its door and is waiting for us. There were lots of discussions and agreements about the country around the world. Including the one in Washington. It was said that our country can embark on the road to Europe. And there is no joking around with Washington. Yes, our country is not large. It is an integral body made up of two pieces.

We are headed towards the place where normal people went long ago. Since this is the case, I started packing to avoid being late, because Europe tolerates no negligence and sloppiness. Indeed, people say I have nothing but worries to bring along. I wonder which path I should take into the world.

Several paths

If I go over Trebevic, which is Sarajevans' favorite picnic site, it could be dangerous. I might run into a minefield ... which means problems ... and Europe will be out of the picture.

If I go over the Goats Bridge, it would take me no time to reach the other entity, which is still doing pretty well. No harm came to it, even from Washington. But, the moment I were to cross the bridge, my chances of running into Cavic would increase drastically, and he could suffocate me with his story about the Republic of Serbia being the creation of the Dayton Accord. I say to myself, I am not going that way either.

If I take the road on the opposite side, I won't be any safer. What if the progressive farmers set up tents on the highway, or, God forbid, scatter potatoes on the road, or lie down on the asphalt. I couldn't continue over the bodies of progressive farmers.

Even the road towards the south is not safe. The Herzegovinian educators could sit down and block the road, as a sign of warning to the authorities, demanding a salary increase and lunch money that they could really use.

They say they will shut down at least 80 schools because of the low salaries. They even cut down on their meals so they could afford buying locks for this purpose. They don't care that we will be an uneducated nation and that we cannot enter Europe as illiterates. We are at the bottom of the chart when it comes to literacy in Europe. The literate ones emigrated, the illiterate ones stayed behind, that's that.

I really don't feel like taking this road to Europe because I might run into Niko Lozancic or Ivo Miro Jovic on their way back from a Croatian Democratic Union meeting in Rama or Livno. Especially Niko, who always attends such meetings, even says something at them. They would bug me with their story about the deprived Croats, about how the Croatian language is neglected in the schools, about the non-existence of a TV station for Bosnian-Herzigovinian Croats....

All I know is that Niko would not bore me with talk about the Federation, which, just for the record, he heads, but it is as if he doesn't. His butt rarely occupies the Federation chair, and he does not often appear publicly as the Federation president. He behaves as if he were the leader of a local community, and not of an entity, the larger one, mind you. The Croatian Democratic Union is more important to him, period! The same way the Party of Democratic Action is much more important to Sulejman Tihic than the country is, or Europe, for that matter. It seems that Tihic only dreams about the disappearance of Republic of Serbia.

It would be best for me to wait a bit. Europe is no rabbit. It will not run away, it could wait some. It would be even better if Karadzic and Mladic were finally captured, and then I could go peacefully into the world. They say that the investigators and Carla Del Ponte are trying, but are failing to track them down.

I know one thing for sure: Radovan is not on an island like Ante Gotovina was. If someone thinks that Radovan is on a beach on the other side of the world drying his underwear, they're mistaken. Bathing is not his strength, he never liked it. You won't see Radovan close to water. Searching for him in monasteries is in vain as well. They've searched them all, and Raso is nowhere to be found. What would he do in a monastery? He would be bored there.

The likelihood is that, as soon as the weather gets better, he would leave his lair, sit under a beech tree, and start playing heroic songs on his gusle (Balkan string instrument). He enjoys the music of his childhood. Raso doesn't know what Canary Islands are about, and why would he go there when there are no gusle to be found? There's no way he's there.

In his life Raso kept trying to do things, but he never succeeded. In his youth he started writing poems, which no one liked, because they didn't even resemble poems. He tried reciting them once, but was booed at the very beginning, because these so-called poems made no sense, and he fled the stage. If Carla had heard them, she would have run away to avoid listening to them.

Sure, many like-minded people are helping him hide. If they found Radovan sleeping under an oak, they wouldn't turn him in, they would bring him tea and a blanket to make sure he doesn't catch a cold for the sake of the vital national interest. This is why I am not surprised that they can't find his lair.

We will export ministers

I find comfort in the fact that we are topping the charts in Europe in one thing. No one can beat us when it comes to the number of governments, ministers, prime ministers, deputies, assistants, advisors, committees, councils, advisory bodies, associations.... We have 180 ministries in this country! Once we start for Europe, we can dump off two-thirds of them in some countries that are lacking various ministers and advisors. Many of them are not that clever, but when in need, they come in handy.

We would like to get rid of them, and, if nothing else, our experts could teach these countries how to spend taxpayers' money, how to use government cars, how to build summer houses, how to collect huge fees for this and that.

The people in the West do not know how to do these things. They are really naïve. They don't even know how to snatch a taxpayer's money, and our guys could teach them how in no time at all.

Our guys are experts in this. In parliaments, in governments, in municipalities.... I am surprised that they haven't figured out how to collect a fat fee for living together with their moms or sisters-in-law. It would do them good.

Much needs to be done before the road to Europe. We would need a broom to clean out the rotten stuff, to install order in the country, to make it look beautiful like a bride before the wedding. Europe is like an old lady courting us, and we keep failing in attempts to charm her.

But, since the right moment came at a bad time, who will do this, and how will it be done? When I analyze the situation a bit, I see that our power-holders are in no hurry to take the country into Europe because they are spending more time abroad than here anyway.

They care more about taking their wives to Europe than their country.

Šefik Dautbegovic*, born in the small town of Prozor, Bosnia and Herzegovina, in 1948; graduated from the Faculty of Political Science in Sarajevo in 1972; worked as a journalist for Oslobodjenje daily in Sarajevo since 1973; worked also for various columns of the newspaper. Currently works as an editor-commentator for Oslobodjenje.*

Novinar Online Daily (www.novinar.net), Bulgaria, 25 July 2007

Bulgaria Online (2007)

By Janina Dragostinova

»Will you write an article about your country for us?«, I was asked by a friend who works in the Austrian media. The proposal in the guise of a question was of the kind of thing to which you can't say no. »Of course I will!«, I replied quickly without much thought. There are situations in life when you first look at your compensation and then you start thinking about how to complete the assignment. Especially when the compensation might possibly be in euros.

Then, however, I did start thinking about it and grasped my situation. Yes, I'd love to write something but I won't be in Bulgaria for two months. I'll be in Germany. No problem, the experienced journalist told me. Our best correspondent for Romania lives in Berlin and writes about Bucharest from there. The world is virtual now. You only need a computer and the Internet and you are everywhere. Long gone are the times of »reports from the place of the event«. Life can be observed online and it is just as exciting.

»Well, if the Romanians are so advanced and modern, what's the point in me refusing?« I said to myself. They can't be any better!

»What are the requirements for the text?« I asked. First, the Austrian explained, it needs to be newsworthy. Second, there has to be a human story behind the news. Third, the story should be characteristic of your country.

But who in Austria cares about my country, I wondered. We in Austria know that Bulgaria and Romania are now part of the EU, the journalist told me. Everything else is a tabula rasa. You can write anything as long as it's interesting, catches the reader's attention and piques his curiosity.

A few days later, I am in Germany. I sit in front of my computer and start searching the Internet for material on a story about my country that portrays its commercial image. In this case, »commercial« means »understandable« to a Western reader. I search in vain. Nothing seems exciting enough to be shared with Austrians. Lots of information about being a new member of the EU. Well, they already know that. My country seems totally lost in the world wide web. The EU, on the other hand, is very active – it gives directives, instructions, it demands one thing, prohibits another ... but Bulgaria is missing. I need to find it. I remember Woody Allen's words that masturbation is also a form of love when it is directed towards a specific person. So I look for Bulgarian realities to embrace them with my online love and sell the to foreigners.

Maybe I should mention here that I am in a European translators' group that is translating the German bestseller *Measuring the World (Die Vermessung der Welt)*. In this book, Alexander von Humboldt goes on endless and exhausting travels in order to measure every peak, hill and river. Was the world an easier place to know in the 18th century, when everything was within reach and mankind was far away from the Internet? I reach the chapter where Humboldt comes back from South America and presents his travel notes. They are packed with tables, numbers and calculations. No adventure, no breathtaking pages. Paris is disappointing, the book says. I'm more relaxed now. So readers then and readers now want the same thing: fewer percentages and more exciting stories. I dive into the Internet again to look for the Bulgarian adventure that will charm the world. It's not possible that there are adventures everywhere but not in Bulgaria. I begin reading in one of the Bulgarian online publications that the government is reporting a decrease in organized crime. This is clearly aimed at Brussels and hardly corresponds to the truth. Our government has already learned that unlike Humboldt's Paris, Brussels does not believe in tears, but in numbers. Only that whatever is good for bureaucrats is boring for readers. Even if dressed up with numbers, the image of my country remains unattractive to the foreign media.

Do you consider Elias Canetti a Bulgarian, the Albanian guy who is translating *Masse und Macht* asks me over dinner. Well,... I reply with uncertainty. Heh-heh, the Albanian laughs. Canetti might have said »Whatever happened to me later I had already lived through in Rustchuk,« but despite that he is not a Bulgarian writer. And don't you dare claim him as yours! It's not enough to be born somewhere to actually be from that place, the Albanian continues. The world is much more complicated than that!

I have no intention of contradicting him. Yes, the world is complex, and somewhere in it my Bulgaria has its place, and I have to find and describe it.

I had saved some money, the Albanian continues. But in the nineties I lost everything in the »pyramids«. Just like in Bulgaria. And now... what can I tell you? Mafia everywhere. Just like in Bulgaria. We have a terrific seaside, but no one goes there anymore. Everyone prefers to go to Greece. The Albanians have raised their prices so much, they want to become rich overnight. Just like in Bulgaria, right?

I nod. I want to tell him that we have the expression »Albanian heater« in Bulgarian to describe somebody who is very slow to understand, but I stop myself because they might have something like a »Bulgarian heater« in their language.

Wherever you go in Eastern Europe, it's all the same, the Hungarian posits. This is why we understand each other with half a word. We don't even need to talk to each other anymore. You say »mutra« or »thick neck« and you understand everything. You say »ex-communists« and you know that they are in power again. No explanations needed. The metaphors – long gone. Life seems mixed, furious, wrapped in thick fog, but it's obvious that we are in the hands of crooks again.

Not really, the Chinese says. There is still ambiguity in language, there is still Aesop's language. In China everybody knows the poem by the great Hungarian poet Sandor Petofi by heart: »I need two things in the world – love and freedom. I would irrevocably sacrifice my life for love, and I would give up my love for freedom.«

This is because you still live in socialism, the Hungarian laughs. You still believe in freedom. We lost our illusions a long time ago. There is no freedom. Or at least the freedom we were all dreaming of. There is only an imitation of democracy and its highest demonstration is the so-called free elections. I am really angry that no one in the West wants to understand that. And they keep working with the old politicians because they know them and are used to them. The people in the West keep investigating the Nazi past of Günter Grass and Martin Walser when they were very young but they don't seem to understand what communism was like. What Petofi, what poetry?!

The Hungarian is visibly angry. The Chinese is trying to calm him down – there is an expression in Chinese, »Bujian busan«, that you say when you are parting with someone. It means »I am here and will be waiting for you until one day you come back to me.«

We will need Asian patience until the European East meets with the European West, the Albanian says and retreats to his Canetti.

Canetti was born in Bulgaria, after all, I whisper to myself, we also have European minds! And I turn to the Internet again. Something may have come up in the meantime.

Here it is: A superior government officer chides a minister that he behaves as if he actually owns the country. There follow promises of investigation and fair punishment. I'm on the right track, I smell a story for sale. It's only human for a man in power to slip up. And to abuse his position. Moreover, the case seems typical for Bulgaria, no doubt about that. I'll wait for the story to unfold and then I will sell it to the Austrians.

Two months later the outcome is still unknown. The minister was removed from government but what he actually did is still a mystery. There are reports that he is now running for another government position. Or that he wants to become mayor of Sofia, and that he won't be giving up his power within his party either. A few days later it is announced that he will head the budget commission in parliament. That was supposedly negotiated when he was removed from government. It is as if he is not there anymore but never actually left.

Bulgarian politicians are like rubber bath toys. They go under the bubbles and then pop up again. But no one dares to throw the dirty water out for fear of throwing the baby out with it. This is why we still bear with them and console ourselves that at least we know these people. Who knows what the new ones will demand? They might be even greedier. On election days we behave like Westerners towards the East, the Hungarian used to say. However, the story about the corrupt politician is hopeless because it has no real end. The papers aren't writing anymore about the promised investigations, let alone fair punishment.

In the meantime, the Greek lady in the Collegium goes to Brussels to meet an Internet friend for the first time. They chatted for months and are now going to see each other. Before the first meeting, the Greek lady is absolutely certain that the World Wide Web is a better world than reality. There is love in the web, there is tenderness, there is adventure. Unfortunately the Belgian online lover turns out to be married. But his wife is nice and gives the Greek lady a gift – a box of expensive Belgian chocolate. The Greek lady is sad that Internet love is as illusionary as real love.

There is nothing left for her but to eat the chocolate that gave her Brussels happiness. It's nice to have been in the EU for a longer time, you seem to swallow grief easier. The Greek lady offers me some chocolate. Sometimes it's fine to have neighbours with more experience with Brussels, even if it is bitter and artificially sweetened.

The Greek lady's Internet disaster encourages me to find some real Bulgarian drama on the web to sell on the media market.

Another shooting in the centre of Sofia in broad daylight. A famous businessman and advisor to the president was shot to death. However, one thing is clear: the case will never be cleared up, so it's useless to concentrate on it. The plot is lost somewhere along the way. Not to mention the fact that people in the West are already fed up with our shootings and investigations that never seem to lead anywhere.

They don't understand who the killers are or what their motives are. If you look at it impartially, organized crime seems like a nightmare in the dreams of a psychopath. It's like a game with no rules whatsoever. So there is no point in writing about it.

One more story catches my eye. Our head of state was a collaborator with the secret service before 1989. We had no real dissidents but as many members of the secret police as you can imagine. So it's no wonder that the president who was part of the majority was one of them. However, the whole story seems a bit foggy. On the one hand he seems to have been a collaborator and there is a dossier to prove that, but there are pages missing from the files and it is not entirely clear whether he should be ashamed of what he did or proud of it. I don't know how I should present him to the Austrian reader. As a complex character who changes depending on the situation? No, no good. I'll have to wait, maybe someday this story will clear up.

Another story: thousands of environmentalists protest in Bulgaria against the destruction of nature, against concrete buildings eating away the Black Sea coast and the mountains. Some authorities finally took their side. But the environmentalists are not happy because the measures are halfhearted. The protests continue.

Doctors protest, too. One day they go on strike, the next day they go to work, but they are fundamentally unhappy. The same is true for teachers. Taxi drivers have been quiet for the past couple of months, but they are always good for revolt. But no protests seem to have a real outcome. There is no story with a final end, there is no full stop anywhere. Bulgaria refuses to be commercially packaged. Everything is a never-ending story in which – contrary to all rules – you cannot understand who the good guys or the bad guys are, or who fights for what. There is crime, but no punishment.

I am on the road for a few days. No Internet. No Bulgaria. My country has disappeared totally as if it never existed. Then it arises again from nowhere – protesting, unhappy, tapping its foot like an angry child, no vision for the future, no idea how to reach the final run. Also full of stories that follow each other, winding, but never reaching a conclusion. Everything at home remains the same, day in, day out ... until the end of the world.

I don't know how the Romanians do it but I give up observing my country from far away. I am failing with the text. No happy end. I intend to go back to Bulgaria and join the protests of people who hate neverending stories. Because how can you tell the story of something that never ends? And most importantly – how can you sell it? Even if we produce countless stories, the fact that they never seem to have an end makes us uncharacteristic enough in the eyes of other Europeans. If you can't add a final note, no one will give you a single euro.

To be continued ... live.

Janina Dragostinova *was born 1962 in Varna, Bulgaria. Today she works as a freelance journalist, writer and translator. Some of her translations from German are:* Die Logik der Bilder *by Wim Wenders,* Anarchie der Phantasie *by Rainer Werner Fassbinder,* Die Reise nach Trulala *by Wladimir Kaminer,* Die

Schattenboxerin *by Inka Parei,* Adler und Engel *by Juli Zeh and* Die Vermessung der Welt *by Daniel Kehlmann. Janina Dragostinova has won several awards and scholarships.*

Tages-Anzeiger Magazine, Switzerland, 24 April 2004

Hungary (2004)

By Miklos Gimes

The friend who collected me from the airport had bought himself a huge estate car. He is making a thoroughly respectable living in film production. His wife works for a private radio station where she has a talk show, one of these programmes where people are looking for a husband or wife. I said that I had read that the Hungarians have the most sex in the world. »I think we are the world champions at boasting if anything«, he said. I asked him to ask his wife whether she could ask listeners for their opinion on Hungary's accession to the EU. Hungary voted for EU accession with an overwhelming majority but the voter turnout was below 50 per cent. Since then pollsters have been racking their brains about what the people really think. »They didn't bother to vote because everybody's in favour of it anyway«, said my friend. Hungary was a member of the Soviet bloc for 44 years because the great powers decided this after the Second World War. Then came the »fall of the wall« and the period of high hopes that now seem to become fulfilled.

The Foreign Ministry in Budapest is on Bem Platz on the Danube, opposite the fairy tale palace that is the parliament building. A grim box from the 19th century, to which a façade reminiscent of a post-modernist third class hotel was added after the wall fell. This is where people demonstrated in huge numbers on 23 October 1956 to demand a democratic Hungary and where the armed uprising broke out the same evening. And very close by, at the back of the ministry, you can find the prison where the insurgents were brought after the Russians crushed the rebellion. I was six years old at the time and my family fled with me to Switzerland. When going through the security checks at the entrance to the building, I had a strange feeling that my life had turned an absurd pirouette.

It was not absurd that Hungary had become a member of the EU but that country had an advantage over Switzerland in something. It was absurd that I wanted to ask the senior civil servant in the Hungarian Foreign Ministry how a small country fares when it wants to join the EU. What do they want in Brussels? How much freedom does a country cede to the EU? And what is this Europe anyway? For decades, Switzerland, which had granted my family asylum, had been for Hungary a political role model, and for me the pivotal point from which I had observed world events, the development of the European Community, the greatest project in post-war western Europe, which was associated with names such as Churchill, Adenauer and de Gaulle.

I was not the only journalist in Budapest who had come from abroad during these April days. The western public seemed curious about the new EU member; it was not interested in the burden of history but in the country's soul, the Hungary beyond the impecunious pensioners, the homeless, the gypsies, the mining towns without work. Their attention was concentrated on the Hungary of the enlightened, aspiring bourgeoisie of the pre-war novels of Antal Szerb and Sándor Márai. A Hungary that had been part of Europe before the Cold War froze this relationship. I was curious about the reciprocal viewpoint, I was interested in the impression that the newcomer had got of Europe during the negotiations. The people I talked to sat in the Foreign Ministry and in the classical Prachstrasse, which leads down to Heldenplatz, in No. 102, where, astounded by the glassy marble air well, one catches sight of the world map with the long list of the offices of Baker & McKenzie, Martonyi és Kajtár. If you reach the offices of Dr. János Martonyi above the gallery on the first floor and face the little old gentleman with the twirled moustache, you can imagine that you have been transported back to a time that could not have been very different sixty or seventy years ago: cosmopolitan and elitist.

János Martonyi was the Foreign Minister in the right wing Fidesz government from 1998 to 2002 and led the negotiations on EU accession, which lasted from 1998 to 2003, until the change of government. He was one of the people I talked to, together with two younger heads of department from the Foreign Ministry who had joined the diplomatic service at the time the wall fell, intelligent, clever men of around 40.

Gábor Iván runs the Economics Department and was a member of the negotiating team in Brussels.

Peter Györkös, who had actually studied in Moscow, is Head of Coordination in the Integration Department, and, as secretary during the accession negotiations, is familiar with every detail of them.

»We arrived at a completely different level of cynicism compared with that at the beginning of negotiations«, said Péter Györkös. »We have learnt our lesson. The most important is that the EU is everything, but not generous. They squeezed everything out of us.« Despite this, all three, Martonyi, Iván and Györkös, are committed Europeans. Not just because they believed that they have done the right thing for their country but because they all – in their own way – see hope in European integration.

Europe means something different for Hungary than it does for Switzerland. »For four decades we were in the wrong place in history«, said Gábor Iván. »If you go to Vienna or to Trieste or to a southern German city, you feel that we belong in the same space. To a part of Europe.«

»What is Europe?«

»It's where there is legal certainty. Where you can buy what you want in shops. Where you can plan your everyday life«, said Iván. Given these needs, Hungary never had any doubts about joining the EU.

»The Union is reputed to be a positive institution here«, said Péter Györkös. »Any country that belongs to it is counted as one of Europe's lucky countries here, but there are still countries like Switzerland or Norway that could join but don't want to. They are very particular countries because they can allow themselves the luxury of standing on their own feet. Hungary cannot afford to do this.«

After 1989 there were two strategic goals for Hungary: the transition to a market economy and integration in the west. »In the last fourteen years we have gone through a process for which there is no instruction manual«, said Gábor Iván. At the same time the changes in the economic system were completed far more rapidly than the process of political integration. Today 65 per cent of Hungary's foreign trade is with EU countries and this figure will rise to 73 per cent following EU expansion. This means that Hungary is already one of the most economically integrated countries in the Union, a model student of free trade. »In terms of custom duties we are as open as EU countries like Denmark or Belgium«, said Gábor Iván. 60 per cent of investment comes from the EU area. The fact that political integration would follow one day was never in doubt but it has taken a long time. »First there was the will to occupy our markets, a process that was completed in the 1990s«, said Gábor Iván. »Today, the vast majority of the Hungarian economy is owned by companies based in western Europe. And because economic integration had already gone so far, there was no particular rush to political integration. Perhaps it's an exaggeration to say that they wanted the markets first and then integration but this is how the process happened. First they wanted to establish branches here and buy up eastern European companies, then they talked to us about eastward expansion. It is therefore difficult to compare our case with Switzerland because the preconditions are so different.«

Hungary's request for admission was accepted by the EU in 1994. Negotiations on accession began four years later, in autumn 1998, together with nine other countries: the three Baltic states, Poland, the Czech Republic, Slovakia, Slovenia, Cyprus and Malta.

»They were not negotiations«, said János Martonyi. »In genuine negotiations two groups sit opposite each other and even if there are serious differences at the start of the discussion, bargaining goes on until the end. But here, it was a matter of Hungary becoming a member of a community with clear rules. The negotiations merely revolved around the extent to which, and the length of time during which, Hungary is permitted to deviate from these rules. To this was added the fact that one side was in a hurry while the other took its time. To start with nothing happened for two years.«

»What could you do to drive the matter forward?«

»Our contribution consisted in convincing the member states to carry out their own resolutions, namely to admit the eastern European countries. We had to become presentable. We had to prove that we are ready.«

»Were there EU countries who were more prepared to accelerate the process?«

»They all said they wanted to support our admission. But what was really important for the Foreign Ministers were the domestic opinion polls on eastward expansion in EU countries. However, geographical proximity was also important. The closer they are, the better they knew us. The greatest breakthrough took place in 2001 under the Swedish presidency. Anne Lindt's commitment to eastward expansion was crucial.«

Early in the 1990s, long before negotiations were thought of, a team of the best people was assembled in the Foreign Ministry. That was the sportier aspect of the matter. »Each of us received a couple of chapters from the EU's acquis communautaire (body of legislation) and then we mugged up on it«, explained Gábor Iván. »Later during the negotiations there were sometimes embarrassing situations because we knew the EU better than the opposite side. It didn't make us exactly popular with everybody.« The opposite side were the EU ambassadors from the fifteen member countries, who had first agreed on a joint position after tough negotiations with each other. »The Union members did not want to talk to us but to each other until they had their standpoint. And changing that was very difficult for us«, said Péter Györkös.

»Basically the negotiations took place between the fifteen?« I asked.

»Absolutely. This is why we had to get involved informally at this level.« The discussions among the member states took place behind closed doors but nevertheless Hungary succeeded in getting information, explained Gábor Iván. »As soon as the fifteen had reached a compromise and the doors opened, they spoke with one voice. Fifteen delegations and we Hungarians, I'm saying this so that you can see what the atmosphere in the room was like: fifteen and one.«

»Like an exam«, I said.

»Exactly like an exam and sometimes they made us feel as though they wanted to find out whether we had done our homework.«

The Union had acted craftily, explained Györkös. »On the question of the free movement of persons, Germany and Austria played the bad guys, while France took on this role on the subject of television and radio broadcasting, and the Austrians in the case of transport. In each case the Union divided the labour involved and confronted us with the toughest attitude to ensure that we did not end up in conflict with all fifteen.« At the same time, it was made clear to Hungary from the beginning that they would be asked to take on the EU's entire body of legislation, the so-called acquis communautaire, in its entirety. There would be no exceptions such as those previously granted to the Danes or the British. The only things that were negoti able were transition regulations in order to allow a soft landing. Hungary proved itself a model student here and has already taken on the acquis communautaire to the extent that corresponds to the EU average. The other side was less cooperative. The EU demanded a transition period of seven years before allowing full free movement of persons; payments to agriculture and for infrastructure are far below the previous EU percentage rate; Schengen is expected to be introduced in 2007. »The eastward expansion was achieved on the cheap«, said János Martonyi. »It cost no more than one per cent of the EU budget.«

The Hungarians were frequently surprised by the pettiness of the Union. »Whether a vet needs six months' practical training for his diploma was such an issue«, said Gábor Iván. »It triggered as much uproar in Brussels as if we had wanted to torpedo the entire project.« Despite this, the Hungarians have kind words for the EU bureaucracy. »The so-called Brussels bureaucracy is a case of mystification«, says Péter Györkös.

»The number of EU civil servants is lower than the administration of Munich. It is nonsense to talk of dictates from Brussels. The people there coordinate and they guide, they look to see whether rules are observed, but execution is a matter for national administrations. The EU determines what a Schengen visa looks like, but the border personnel and consulates are not managed from Brussels.«

If anything it was the dictate of unconditional affiliation that opened the eyes of the Hungarian negotiators. »From time to time I asked myself why they treated us like this«, said Gábor Iván. »There are 1,500 cases at the European Court of Justice,where member countries have breached EU rules, and they demanded one hundred per cent obedience from us.«

»Has this attitude anything to do with the fact that you are the poor relations from the east? Or must all new members expect this intransigence from now on?« I asked.

»I think there's a little of both. The fact that we are poor relations certainly played a role. The EU countries talk differently to Switzerland, this is clear from the bilateral discussions. If you think about how they dealt with us, it leaves an unpleasant taste«, said Gábor Iván.

»Was Hungary too ready to compromise? Did you have too little self-confidence?« I asked the former Foreign Minister.

»There was no lack of self-confidence«, said Martonyi. »But the message was clear: take it, or leave it. It was we who wanted to join the club, we had knocked on the door but it is they who admit you. It would have required great cohesion among the ten accession countries to have negotiated better conditions.«

The Hungarians were able to mug up and be model students as they wanted, but in the end their accession conditions were decided on ground on which their influence was limited: in negotiations with Poland.

The EU's strategy of eastward expansion was focused on Poland; the fact that the negotiations were led by Günter Verheugen, a German, was not a matter of chance. Poland is the giant among the ten accession countries. The Poles account for half the 75 million new EU citizens. Poland's antiquated infrastructure and its large farming community posed the greatest risk for the EU's budget. And the Union's fears of being swamped with cheap labour are associated with Poland. At the same time, surveys undertaken by the EU show that no mass migration, even from Poland, is to be expected. There, some three per cent of people over the age of fifteen, especially well-educated, younger people without families, are thinking of emigrating. In the accession countries as a whole, the number of potential migrants falls to one per cent. A new picture in the history of European migration: it is no longer the rural poor, who will one day want to bring their families over, that are surging into western Europe, as they once did from Mediterranean countries. Specialists agree that this wave of migration, if it happens, will constitute a greater problem for the accession countries with their low birth rates than for the host countries, whose economies can use educated young people. The long transition period for the free movement of persons has less to do with economic rationality than with western European politicians' consideration for the fears of their unemployed electorates.

The experience of the Polish hegemony has prepared Hungary for everyday life in the EU. »It is not a particularly pleasant feeling, being a small country in the Union«, said Gábor Iván. »My Danish colleagues have often told me of their frustrations. The Danes are very active but they have few votes in Council meetings and the large countries imply that they have little to say. If the big three, Germany, France and the UK, are united, then they determine the course. It is not a matter of chance that attempts are now being made to prevent the large countries from making decisions alone.« Since the accession treaties were signed over a year ago, and the Hungarians are presented in every body as observers, they have got to know the shop from inside. »It is unbelievable how the partners speak to each other. They blackmail each other in meetings«, said Gábor Iván. »They go straight for the jugular even in questions that obviously relate to the interests of the Union as a whole.«

»Is there no sense of any common political will then?« I asked.

»Yes, the political will is there, but it needs a great deal of pressure from outside«, said Iván. »That was clear at the summit meeting last March. Following the Madrid attack everybody wanted to show unity, everybody spoke of political union, which advanced the discussion about the constitution slightly. These attempts happen again and again but Europe remains a Europe of nation states.«

What is the European Union? A utopia? An economic operation? Or simply the lowest common denominator of what will shortly be twenty-five nations? I had to travel to Budapest before I realised that the EU is the legacy of European history. It is not a messianic utopia like the United States of America. Europe's past is too bloody, too tattered, too chaotic for that. No, the EU is a project to continue the old European spats, only shots are no longer fired.

He was an old man of sixty, said János Martonyi with determined breeziness. For his generation, European integration meant more than for a thirty year old. »Forty years ago I would never have been able to imagine that there would be such a thing. There must be something there, a feeling of belonging together, that you could describe as a European identity.«

»And how far are you down the road to European integration?« I asked.

»Half way. The last fifty years were successful, the question is whether the next fifty will also be successful. Integration and disintegration are processes that always work simultaneously. In my opinion the road is passable. The world is moving in the direction of new centres, Europe could join in. The greatest risk for Europe is national power games when it is only a matter of bringing the national viewpoint to bear.«

Europe is a large community, said Péter Györkös, which must unite many interests. »One sometimes has to concede, otherwise everything grinds to a halt. The EU is a structure that can only move forward. Even standing still signifies a crisis.«

»Does an expanded Europe mean even more Europe?« I asked.

»Undoubtedly«, said Györkös. »Many do not want to see it that way but if you think that an idea that six countries once thought up now applies to a area covered by twenty-five countries, it is not a minor issue. There will be changes and reforms, there will be diverging interests, but it can also be an opportunity.«

»For a Europe with a new face?«

»This new Europe will not be as new as many people think. Anybody who thinks this underestimates the ability of the new members to adjust. The societies of the accession countries are more resilient than those of the old EU. What hasn't changed since 1989? Every month brings changes. Everyday life changes from day to day. People have become a bit comfortable in the old countries. No, the major changes will not be the result of eastward expansion, but of globalisation, and we cannot suppress these processes. Comfortable societies tend to suppress. In the long term that is not a good policy. In this respect the accession countries can bring a great deal to the Union because we are more flexible and better able to adapt.«

»Do you have any children?« I asked.

»Yes, a girl in the third form«, said Györkös.

»What will she get from what you have been working for for the last ten years?«

»The fact that in a few years it will be immaterial whether she was born in Budapest or Göteborg or Lisbon. Our standard of living will always be lower than that of Germany for example. But the opportunities are more important. The horizon.«

»Will there be losers?«

»Agriculture will have problems because it is not competitive, but that has nothing to do with the EU.

»This will also be true for certain branches of industry such as the textile sector and heavy industry. For these people it is a tragedy but those are laws of economy.«

The EU? Not bad

As my friend drove me back to the airport, I asked him what listeners had said to his wife about the EU.

»I wrote a couple of things down for you«, he said. »A fifty-year-old said, ›We are now paying for it but our children will benefit from it.‹ A young woman said, ›It was obvious. Nothing else was conceivable.‹ Another young woman said, ›Ask me in ten years.‹«

My friend is a few years older than Péter Györkös. His father was involved in the uprising in 1956, which meant that his family was subsequently repeatedly victimised. »What do you actually think of the EU?« I asked him.

»The EU? Not bad«, he said. But what I don't understand is why we have to join something else again. We were under the Soviets for forty years, then we broke away and now we have to throw ourselves at another power. Couldn't we do our own thing for once?«

***Miklos Gimes**, born 1950 into a family of staunch communists, who later renounced communism and played a key role in the 1956 revolution in Hungary. His father, Miklos Gimes, was executed in 1958 as a part of the trial of Imre Nagy. Escaped with his mother to Switzerland, where he studied economics. Reporter for the* Zürcher Tages-Anzeiger *since 1985. Gimes is also involved in filmmaking:* Elf Freunde *(1998; Arte; Festival Duisburg),* Mutter *(2002; Festivals: Berlinale, Viennale, Lincoln Center).*

Capital weekly, Issue 21, Bulgaria, June 2005

Frau Bulgarin, Ivan Milev and Gustav Klimt (2005)

»Die Vergangenheit war noch nie so schön wie heute.« From a poster in the Cafe das möbel, Vienna.

By Diana Ivanova

The first story I hear from anyone in Vienna is about a woman without a name – she was simply Frau Bulgarin, Mrs. Bulgarian. Suzanne tells me the story while we are having lunch at the Institute for Human Sciences. Her voice is full of loving nostalgia: »Many years ago there was a Bulgarian restaurant at the Guertel roundabout near the Gumpendorfstrasse metro station in the 15th District. Rila, it was called. This woman, Frau Bulgarin, was the spirit of the restaurant. I never knew her name. She was always in a hurry, never quite happy with her customers' orders and she dropped the plates on the tables with a bang.... She always wore an apron to wipe her hands on. The place was grim and old-fashioned but we all went there because of this grumpy woman – she served the best food in the world at the lowest prices.... But the restaurant is no longer there....«

When I travel in Western European countries I see that the us-and-them division really exists. I always know when I am in Western Europe – the feeling of nostalgia is not forbidden there.

I have my own theory about being a successful Bulgarian expat – it is how good you are at translating your nostalgia for your forbidden past to them, the people in the West. You are successful if you use these forbidden feelings to your advantage. You are not if you shut them in and become their victim.

A year ago I met Kinga, a Hungarian from Budapest, at a seminar in Austria. She told me: »It's just great that I don't have to explain everything to you – communism, democracy – there is no end to it, I use so much energy in explanations. You and I can simply talk without these explanations and you know exactly what I mean....«

I am no longer surprised when I meet West Europeans who know nothing about Bulgaria. It's happened so many times that it's no longer a problem. I don't even have a desire to explain anymore. I simply accept reality, just like Kinga.

But what surprised me in Vienna is that there are plenty of people who know nothing about Slovakia and have not once been to the capital, Bratislava, forty minutes away on the train.

Elizabeth is in her late twenties, a web designer at a software company on Mariahilferstrasse. Wolfgang is 37, an architect, born in Bodensee, Germany. He has lived in Vienna for 12 years. Neither of them has been to Bratislava. At the Institute for Human Sciences I meet other people who have been to Slovakia just once in the last 15 years.

Austria and Slovakia are divided by the Danube but have a common future now – both are members of the European Union. What many people in either country have yet to discover is that there is more than the river that divides them – their memories, their pasts are different. Could it be that these memories can also be points of unification? This question comes to me after I talk with two more people who have rarely or never been to Eastern Europe.

Michael Staudigal and Astrid Svenson know little about Bulgaria. Instead of trying to fill in the gaps in person, I give them the address of a website which I have recently put together with a group of colleagues in Bulgaria. The website, www.spomeniteni.org, is a growing collection of personal stories about Bulgaria's communist period posted by people of different age and background.

Michael is a lecturer in philosophy at the University of Vienna and a post-doctoral student at the Austrian Academy of Sciences. The effect of our website on him surpasses my expectations. After reading some of the stories Michael tells me that for the first time he has a feeling that he understands something about his neighbors, the Slovaks. » Our knowledge [about Slovakia] was very general. We know that [during the communist period] there was the intelligentsia and the common people. We used to walk along the Danube and Morava and what we saw of Slovakia was a poor wasteland. There were no ordinary people in sight, just soldiers. And factories. This was our image of the country. We never had any details. But it is exactly the details that make all the difference. There was a sense of fear because these soldiers were only 50 meters across the river from us....«

Astrid Svenson is German, a Ph. D. student in history at Cambridge University. The Bulgarian website stories bring back memories from her childhood. She was born in 1977 in Cologne. Her family has successively lived in the Netherlands, France and Belgium. Eastern Europe for her was »as far away as Asia«. She was 12 when the Berlin Wall fell. »I remember a long summer evening in France. My parents were discussing Gorbachev, perestroika, and glasnost with friends who were over for dinner, while I was destroying a bowl of chocolate teddy bears. My father explained to me that this was not a polite thing to do in front of our guests.«

»At school communism was simply absent from out textbooks – with the exception of the *Commu-*

nist Manifesto, the movement from the 1930s and the Weimar Republic – all heroic images. It wasn't until later that I realized that the history books and the discussions at home had made me internalize a great contradiction: communism in the 1930s was a good thing but communism after 1945 was a bad thing.« There was little on post-war Germany in Astrid's history books. »I had a great history teacher but even she had a strange explanation about it: ›The two parts of Germany have now reunited so there is no more need to discuss their history.‹« At the time Astrid accepted this statement but when she went to the university and met with students from Eastern Europe, she realized how influenced her thinking was by Cold War rhetoric. She became more and more interested in recent European history and in the place of her own memories in it. Astrid saw herself in one of the Bulgarian stories on www.spomeniteni.org – the story of a Bulgarian man who went on a trip to Western Europe and discovered how provincial and isolated his own country was. »This is how I feel when I go back home to Cologne,« Astrid continues. »I've had the privilege to be able to travel ever since I was a child.

»And I always feel the same way when I go back to my parents' home in a middle-class suburb outside Cologne. There is no excitement whatsoever; life has no pulse in Cologne. I had the same feeling when I returned to my university in Mainz after two years in France. Berlin is the only place that's different in Germany.«

When we part, Astrid is grateful for the stories »you've given me«. They've reminded her of long-forgotten words, images and smells, and she has shown her feelings to me. I am grateful too.

The Alchemy of Nostalgia

It seems to me that Europe has a trap for Eastern Europeans. If they stay in Eastern Europe, they feel nostalgic for their communist past. If they move to Western Europe, they deny themselves the right of memory and this opens the door to melancholy. It's painful and there is no easy way around it – I've spoken to many Eastern Europeans who feel the same way. The key is perhaps in the words of Eva Hoffman, author of the novel *Lost in Translation*, who wrote after she immigrated to the United States: »To a certain extent you need to rewrite your past to be able to understand it.... If you've been cut away from certain parts of it, you tend to see it either through the veil of nostalgia – which is an ineffective relationship with your past, or through the veil of alienation – which is an ineffective relationship with your present....«

Havelka Café

I keep thinking while I am in Vienna that if you don't have your own kind of nostalgia, you need to invent it. I am surprised to see layers of nostalgia in the Havelka Café.

Any Viennese will be willing to show it to you. The place is barely lit, the chairs squeak, the upholstery is old. But Havelka is full of people. Mr. Havelka is at the door showing his guests in. Mrs. Havelka died a few months ago, so you can no longer order her home-made sausages and pastries. People come here to talk to each other. There is no music in the old Viennese cafés and all you can hear are the conversations.

Havelka brings back to my mind the story of Frau Bulgarin, the grumpy woman with the stained apron. It's the most authentic story about a Bulgarian immigrant anybody ever told me in Vienna. The questions keep coming: Why have we buried these stories, why are we running away from our past?

Havelka is about nostalgia, you can savor all its nuances here. Nostalgia is made up of *nostos* – return, and *algia* – pain. There must be two types of nostalgia. One insists on *nostos*, on return. It is the dangerous type, the one that makes you oblivious of the present. The other, the curative type, insists on *algia* – on reconnecting with pain and accepting it as an existential inevitability. It was St. Luke who said: »Pain is a story that exists in the whole world.«

Ivan Milev, Adriana Czernin and Gustav Klimt

In Vienna I also meet with Adriana Czernin, a successful Bulgarian artist who has lived in the Austrian capital since 1990. Adriana is another person who makes me think that the »translation« from »our« language into »their« language is yet to happen. That East and West are still divided.

I come across Adriana's works at the prestigious Albertina Museum, as part of the exhibition Seven Women – Contemporary Austrian Art (October 2004 – April 2005). I look at her paintings and I think I recognize that she, like me, is also trying to reconnect to an elusive, nebulous past. Her work reminds me of my own fears: that I have no common »Balkan« memories with the Serbs (see Prague: Hermelin and Depression), that my memories of communism are different from those of the Czechs and the Slovaks, that my nostalgia for the past has nothing in common even with the feelings of my own fellow countrywomen (see Lyutenitsa, Rholik and Vaclav Havel). I fear that I've been left alone with my own memories and that I will be able to make sense of them only if I go through them one by one. Only then will I be able to connect to other people.

I really enjoy talking with Adriana Czernin after seeing the show. She was born in 1969, just a year after me, and I find we have a lot in common. She also tells me a story that I am not sure what to think about. Here it is.

Many of the critical reviews of her work compare it to the Jugendstil and particularly to Gustav Klimt. I ask her if this is intentional.

»Not really. But there is an interesting story behind it. Someone who has had a great influence on my style is the Bulgarian painter Ivan Milev. He is completely unknown here but he created his own, very personal version of Jugendstil in Bulgaria 10–15 years after the style was introduced in Vienna. I really admire his work. I used to have a book with reproductions of his paintings which at the time I studied with great attention. I was fascinated by the decorative elements, the interplay between foreground and background which confuses you and makes it impossible to tell which is which. Years later when I saw Klimt's works in Vienna I thought that Ivan Milev had more force, more tragic energy than Klimt and that Klimt's paintings are somehow more decorative. So if there is a connection of my works to Klimt, it is through Ivan Milev.... Curiously, when I started painting in this style in Vienna no one thought to compare them to Klimt.

»But someone made this comment in the United States, where I took part in an exhibition of contemporary Austrian artists at Mass MOCA, Massachusetts. And the Austrian media picked it up.«

I ask her, if she has told anybody – the journalists, the critics – in Austria anything about Ivan Milev. »Not really.« »No one is interested?« »I don't know....« she replies.
This is what confuses me – Ivan Milev has been replaced by Gustav Klimt and this affected no one, absolutely no one. Why?

***Diana Ivanova**, born 1968 in Bulgaria, studied journalism and mass communication in Sofia, Bulgaria, and cultural anthropology as well as art management in Salzburg, Austria. She worked as a radio and TV journalist and was awarded a Bulgarian prize for best TV short presentation in 1993. Together with the Swiss artist Eli Geiser, she exhibited the multimedia installation »Melody of the East« in Basel and Sofia in 2004, and the »Poetry installation« in Prague and Sofia in 2003.*

Capital weekly, Issue 23, Bulgaria, June 2005

Polish Sauna (2005)

By Diana Ivanova

Vienna-Katowice-Wroctaw

The moment you enter Poland everything changes abruptly as though a silent order has been issued – the whole train is filled with people, lots of them, who look hard for a vacant space in the compartments and the corridors, I can feel their clothes against my body, a smell of rain, woolen vests, bread. All the seats in my compartment have been taken, we are sizing up each other, a woman is knitting, an elderly couple is taking sandwiches wrapped in newspaper from a plastic bag, I am trying to read a book in German, which arouses curiosity, and some of my neighbors try to see the title. A little before Wroctaw, the woman sitting next to the woman with the knitting asks whether I will be sitting for an examination in German, because she is one of the examiners. I smile and shake my head: No, I won't be. The Vienna-Katowice-Wroctaw train is almost an exact copy of the Sofia-Vratsa-Vidin train – the »fat train« as it was called – which I often used as a student, a train of »No Distances between People«. I smile because I can feel familiar things coming.

18 in 1989

How does it feel to be born and live in Wrocław, to have been 18 in 1989 when communism collapsed, to belong to the »generation of winners«, as it is called? It feels very, very lonely, says Kamilla, who was born in the 70s and has just completed a dozen interviews with people from this category. Kamilla does not suspect that her answer comes as no surprise to me. I myself belong to the same group even though my geography is different. But of course, I am curious, I want to know more. Kamilla is a sociologist and is working on her doctoral thesis on »post-communism as an experiential category and the viewpoint of today's 30-year-old Poles« – the Poles who were 18 in 1989. Why did she choose them? »I wanted to talk to people who grew up during the socialist period and whose system of values was shaped in the 1980s. Besides, these people are said to be the ›generation of the winners‹. When they started their careers and adult lives at the beginning of the '90s there was an urgent need for highly educated specialists on the labor market. It is said that they had opportunities like no other generation before or after them. Personally I think that this is something of a modern myth, so it was interesting to see whether they consider themselves fortunate. And I have to tell you, after all these interviews, that they feel very lonely.

They are different from the elderly and different from those who were born in the '80s because they no longer remember anything from the socialist past – the queues for everything, the food rations and the endemic shortages in the shops. Interestingly, no one mentions the censorship, the limited liberties, what they all talk about is the queues....«

The »helpers« and the »managers«

The people that Kamilla talked to are all from Wroctaw. She divides them into two groups – the »managers« who run a business, and »the helpers« – those who help other people (homeless, tramps, beggars, refugees, orphans, etc.). Most of them started out as volunteers and then moved on to a full-time job.

When they talk about Poland, the »managers« use the singular »I« and never the plural »We«. With the »helpers« it is the other way round.

»The helpers« in Poland are a very large group, as I was able to see for myself during my stay. All my friends and acquaintances were, at some point in their lives, volunteers. They all talk about Ukraine, the Orange Revolution, and about the need to help Ukraine become a member of the European Union. Poland is the country which sent the largest number of foreign volunteers and observers during the elections in the Ukraine, and most of them were very young. This prompted many media to start talking about the rise of a new active civil population which continues the positive tradition of Solidarity in a new direction and with a different style.

»Solidarity«, the soul, vodka, Chopin

»Solidarity« is a controversial word in Poland, especially after the failed government by the movement's political wing in 1997–2001, but it is a name familiar to all. Solidarity is a story told and re-told. There is, for example, an interesting story about the new logo of the country.

Shortly before its accession to the European Union, Poland acquired a new logo designed to reflect the new image and rebirth of Poles. The logo is a merry kite and the name »Polska« in the typical and unmistakable characters of Solidarity. In the process of looking for images, one of the big advertising companies in Poland asked expatriates in Poland to list the words with which they associate Poland. The result was: Solidarity, Chopin, grey and cold, poor, vodka, kielbasa, Catholics, Walesa, conservative, reform, anti-Semitism, Auschwitz, pollution, soul, romantic.

It emerged that apart from Solidarity and the idea of freedom, Poland has practically no recognizable symbols in the outside world. This is why the new logo reflects the style of something familiar and adds to it something new – the kite as a symbol of individual freedom, romanticism, openness, the soul.

My visit to Poland was shortly before the 25th anniversary of Solidarity, the first independent trade union in the Eastern bloc – it was due to be celebrated in August. I remember that back then, this was the first time I had felt genuine excitement around me in Bulgaria. There was a joke in the '80s: a woman in a crowded tram asks, »Are there no men here to offer me a seat?« Answer: »All the men are in Poland« I realize too that this story never ceased to exist, that if you want to live today there is no way you can ignore it, and that your only chance, given at this moment, is to understand its relevance for you.

The positive things

Kamilla showed her interviewees eight photographs from the 80s and 90s (an empty shop from the 80s, the Pope during his second visit to Poland, the Round Table, Lech Walesa, martial law, Kwasniewski) and let them talk. She thinks she can detect similarities in the way young Poles talk: they refuse to talk about the Pope, refrain from insulting Walesa, confuse their personal memories with the collective ones (for example, many people say they saw tanks on the streets, even though in most cases they are reporting the words of other people). An important point: they feel the need to remember positive things and even insist on them. One of her interviewees even accused her of sensationalism and refusing to see »the good things about socialism – the glass of milk that was served in schools, the subsidized holidays, the summer camps....« But I've been thinking about this too, Kamilla says. »When I look at the pictures from that time, my life during the 80s and my parents, what do I see? Is this socialism? When I look at pictures taken today what I see is not democracy but the grubby streets, the shabby people, my country.«

I ask her whether her interviews changed in any way her own views of socialism, of life then and today. She does not hesitate. »Yes, now I know that socialism is not over yet. We are not citizens yet. We take too many things for granted. Socialism remains deeply entrenched in the way we think and explain reality – we see the social sphere in terms of ›us‹ (society) and ›them‹ (the politicians, the government), and have no sense that we could make a difference, that we have a responsibility to our community. We live in grubby, ugly cities because we don't care. We refuse to understand that there isn't anybody else but ourselves.«

Tea with jam and God

The only taste that stays with me from Wrocław is that of tea with jam served in a small glass bowl, *konfitura porzeczkowa*, in the cosy cafe K2 on Kietbasniczka Street. As we walked through the city with the canals – my friends said that only Venice and

Amsterdam have more canals – I saw a restaurant called »Czech Film« and I asked what that meant. My friends laughed, »When we want to say that something is totally obscure, we call it a Czech film«.

More tea with jam (this time it is *konfitura pomerancova*) and we talk about religion, God, Catholicism.

I remember this: »I would go and confess very often; for me the Church was everything until the day when the priest interrupted my confession and said, ›Young lady, why don't you find yourself a shrink?‹«

Wrocław/Breslaw/ Krzyzowa/ Kreisau

I am trying to imagine what it is like to live in a place where everything has two names and two histories. I am not sure I am succeeding. It seems to me that this kind of thing creates an invisible sensitivity to history, which is characteristic of the Poles, for whom every narrative has a natural historical twist. There is no need to steer the conversation in that direction, it takes that turn naturally. I am not surprised that Wroctaw has preserved a tradition which disappeared in Prague a long time ago and, according to one of my Polish hosts, Irek, is one of the best things about the city – every evening a man on a bicycle lights up the street gas lanterns in the old town.

It seems to me, however, that I am beginning to understand the change of city names as a painful process which is more likely to alienate than befriend you and that to avoid this, you must promise the city to tell it both stories. I now see the change of names of so many Bulgarian cities after 1989, including my home town Mihailovgrad-Montana, in a totally different way: as an alchemical process seeking more to invite you to commiserate with them in their pain than to forget the pain, to embrace rather than reject it.

Sauna in Krzyzowa

In the small village of Krzyzowa on the outskirts of Wroctaw I discover the Kreisau Circle/Der Kreisauer Kreis – a group of intellectuals during the Nazi period who had the intellectual courage to stand up to the regime because it was obvious to them that what was happening in Germany was »devastating not only for the cities, but in an even more horrible way for people's hearts and minds«. The group tried to find the spiritual routes to help after the evil had struck and met in the mansion of Helmut James von Molke in the village which was then called Kreisau. Most of them were killed in 1944 or 1945. After the Second World War, Kreisau became Polish Krzyzowa and in the place of the mansion a socialist farm was built. The end of communism in 1989 gave rise to a joint Polish-German initiative to restore the place as a Foundation for European Understanding where young people from different European countries meet. (See www.krzyzowa.org.pol.)

So I went, invited by my friend Agnieszka who had started work there a few months before. One of the first things we did was to visit the sauna at night and then take a walk in the cold outside when everybody was asleep and the only sound came from the flock of crows. Then we took a tour of the Kapelenberg Cemetery, the Molke castle with its veranda for conversations, the permanent exhibition of the history of opposition against all totalitarian regimes in Europe in the 20th century – national socialism and communism. Needless to say, Bulgaria does not feature in this exposition. This is not surprising but it makes me see something else: Bulgaria is absent not only from the minds of western Europeans (as Michael and Astrid tell me in Vienna – see »Frau Bulgarin«) but from the map of Eastern Europe's history of freedom. None of my friends associates Bulgaria with »freedom« but more with pleasant things such as the lapping of the sea and delicious food. We are not on the map of freedom but on the map of smells. Irek remembers his parents saying after a visit to the Black Sea coast that Bulgarians have a higher standard of living than the Poles, but he cannot unearth a single fact about Bulgaria's recent history from his head. He finds his ignorance interesting and starts questioning me. We had a long midnight conversation about this. We realized that we had both taken it too much for granted that just because our systems were the same, everything else was too. In fact it is not. Both Irek and Agnieszka are very much interested in finding out how things actually were and what legacy we have received. We are chatting away about all this as though we have known each other for years.

Wroctaw and Krzyzowa may be cold and grey, but I leave feeling warm, and for the first time I am ready to subscribe to the cliché of the Slavic soul.

Capital weekly, Issue 19, Bulgaria, May 2005

Prague Hermelin and Depression
(WINNER 2005)

By Diana Ivanova

»How are you?« I ask. »*Mam depku*«, Karolina replies and reminds me of one of the most common expressions in the Czech Republic. It means »I have a small depression«.

»Mam depku« is one of the sweetest Czech expressions. It's a friendly wink at depression.

»Mam depku« is a good test for foreigners and expats in Prague. They are on a journey to find a world without pain and they are surprised to hear all this talk about depression in the middle of Golden Prague.

The Czechs have their questions too. Why all the talk about a »transition period«, if »Mam depku« is still one of the most common expressions? Why should everyone be subjected to the change from communism, to post-communism, to democracy, if no one can be any more sure of their place in this process than before?

In the 1970s, in one of his famous open letters to Czechoslovakia's then-president Gustav Husak, dissident Vaclav Havel wrote: »Little by little we are losing our sense of time. We are beginning to forget and to confuse the chronology of events. We feel that it's all the same after all. This feeling is suffocating us.« In 1989 a more optimistic Havel said: »Time has re-emerged. It's as if we are back in history.«

But 15 years later it doesn't take to be an intellectual to know that for Eastern Europe there is no such thing as being going back to a »clean« history. History is your history and mine. Or to put it more directly – Prague, Bratislava, Brussels and Sofia have different histories and remember different things.

Isn't that a good enough reason for depression?

In 1997, I loved touring the expensive new restaurants opening up across Prague – French, Scandinavian, Thai and Arabic. I loved going to Doli Bel, the pub owned by Kusturitsa's friend Vesso Jorem, where my friends and I drank Montenegrin wine for long, noisy hours. We used to laugh at the Czech who went to the cheap and smelly Zizkov and Holesovice pubs where draft beer and hermelin (Czech cheese) were the luxury items We liked to pontificate that no one can escape the damage of communism. We lived in a Prague of our own – golden, elitist, coldly post-communist. The good-hearted but smelly part of town was dangerous, too full of reasons for nostalgia. Then Vesso Jorem sold Doli Bel, opened a new pub, Gitanes, and grew more and more nostalgic (»Yugoslavian socialism was the best kind, it was the greatest time in history«). It was about then that I started to realize that our Balkan memories were not the same, and nostalgia means different things for each of us. It made me fearful in a strange atavistic way.

The transition period is propaganda

»The ›transition period‹ is propaganda.« This statement was made by SAMISEBE, one of the most unconventional sociological projects in Central Europe.

»SAMISEBE is a revolt against mainstream sociology«, says Rudolf Schmidt, a photographer in his early 50s who works in the field of visual sociology and has, among other things, photographed scarecrows for the past ten years.

In 1991, eight sociologists born between 1924 and 1963 founded the SAMISEBE (Our Own Selves) Association and began researching and recording their own life histories from the socialist period. They decided to turn their biographies into databases and reflect on them together. »The [official] history was full of inadequate concepts and schemes which had nothing to do with our own life experiences«, says Zdenek Konopasek, now editor of Biograph Magazine.

For five years the eight sociologists subjected themselves to a permanent workshop in which they recorded numerous autobiographical stories. They used different themes. One such theme was the various homes they had lived in during the period and the circumstances that had brought them to live there. »Every Sunday my husband and I would go to his parents' place for Sunday lunch, to make ends meet. At the time I didn't like that and it's only now that I see that my parents-in-law were pleased to be making a contribution to our life and that it made them feel they were needed.« Another theme was everyone's life between 7 and 9 in the morning. »My sister and I used to let the dog come to our bed in the morning. I vaguely remember that one day my parents found that the quilt was torn to pieces. They were not pleased.«

Stories were also collected about the meaning of the communist party for each of the authors. »When I was shouting ›Glory to the Party‹ and ›Long Live the Party‹ at demonstrations, I had no idea that the Pioneers' organization [of which I was a member as a child] was related to the communist party.«

The message of this Czech experiment is that our past and present are interrelated, that post communism is rooted in communism, and that the definitive farewell to our communist past is simply not happening.

»You would think that the ›transition period‹ is a way of connecting the past and the present, of transforming communism into post-communism. But in practice, the ideology of our time isolates the present from the past and distorts the relationship.

»Our autobiographical approach makes up for this. It draws the attention to apparently insignificant details [of our past]. The more fragile and intangible they are, the more important they are to us.

»We don't think the definitive farewell to our communist past in the name of the great transformation of Eastern Europe is happening.

»We have every reason to believe that the people, words and things in our ›societies in transformation‹ should be traced to a variety of ages, genres and styles.«

Ruhla Watches

Ruda, as Rudolf Schmidt is known among friends, is a wonderful cook and likes to tell stories about scarecrows. The first thing he remembers when we start talking about socialism is Ruhla watches, formerly made in the German Democratic Republic. He remembers the humiliating customs checks performed by the Czech authorities on the Czech-German border – the watches were illegal imports in Czechoslovakia, as were Salamander shoes. I, too, have a story with Salamander shoes. In 1984, upon return from my first German language camp in Schmalkalden, I triumphantly brought no less than three pairs of Salamanders to Bulgaria. Different stories, different genres and styles.

The SAMISEBE project was a harbinger of a true »reflective« revolution which is sweeping through the Czech Republic. The revolutionary media are film, the Internet and oral history. I discuss Jan Hrebejk's recent films with Vesselin Vachkov, Editor-in-Chief of Lidove Noving. He says Hrebejk's films make use of »therapeutic nostalgia«: »These are the most successful [Czech] films of our time. They are set in the 1960s and the 1980s – Pelisky, Pupendo ... The Czechs call them *laskava comedie*, loving satires – there is a sense in them that our lives were sad, absurd and unbearable but they are also worth a laugh.«

Another clear sign of »revolutionary« upheaval comes from the book publishing world. In 2004 »In the Labyrinth of the Revolution« by political historian Jiri Suk received the prestigious Magnezia Litera Award and became the talk of the whole country. Suk, born in 1966, was surprised by his book's success and by the fact that there were no heated discussions of his main arguments, i.e., that the so called Velvet Revolution of 1989 was completely chaotic and that no one was ready for it; the best prepared were the members of the communist elite, the least prepared were the dissidents. These arguments were not new but Suk substantiated them with numerous facts and documents and this is what makes his work ground-breaking.

These arguments are also supported by the work of the five-year-old Centre for Oral History in Prague. The Centre has recently funded two large-scale research projects . One of them, called »A hundred Student Revolutions«, studied the student demonstrations of 1989; the other recorded the family histories of Czech dissidents and communist party functionaries. »The truth is that Czech society never had communist and dissident ghettos as many people now believe. There were numerous small islands of freedom where people lived as best they could. These people were not heroes, they did not listen to Radio Free Europe, but they didn't collaborate with the regime either. It is also true that Czech dissidents did not find an appropriate language to speak to these [ordinary] people«, says Miroslav Vanek, Director of the Centre.

Why do we need new interpretations of the past?

Paradoxically or not, the current president of the Czech Republic, Vaclav Klaus, is also part of this new wave of post-communist reflection. »I absolutely don't agree with the idea that communist society was made of two distinct ingredients: a small group of heroic rebels and the rest of the people – the collaborators«, he says in an interview in Hospodarske Novini in November 2004. »It simply wasn't like that. We need to be looking not just at the intentions of the communist party but at the reality of the system. The two were diametrically different. I spent 48 years of my life during socialism and I was actively observing the political process throughout most of them. I don't share this view of communist society. Communism was a social system with a life of its own. It wasn't an asteroid which came from the skies and brought about unseen, unexpected changes. Although we did not have any modern analytical literature to help us in the process, we studied various dictatorial regimes of the past and tried to make sense of our own system through them ... We were greatly inspired by the Spanish philosopher Ortega y Gasset and his book *The Revolt of the Masses*, written before the time of communism and fascism. When I read it, I thought it gave a fair description of the foundations of our system.«

Of course, there are those who are suspicious of the motifs behind this view: »Klaus is saying this to counterbalance the gravitational field that Havel still generates despite his withdrawal from active politics. Klaus also made a few small concessions to the communists during his presidential campaign which helped him win the presidency. But the fact that he is talking about the socialist period, the very fact of this discussion is good«, says Vesselin Vachkov.

Martin Smok is a documentary film maker. He is my age, 37. I met him at a party in a friend's apartment in Vinohradi. He worked as a senior consultant at Steven Spielberg's Visual History Foundation in Los Angeles for two years before returning to the Czech Republic. »I came back because I had work here but also because I did not understand the way people live in L.A. I thought I was on Mars, I simply didn't know what was going on around me. My time in L.A. changed the way I view myself and I realized I needed to live in Prague. I understand the people here. People in the West don't have the kind of memories and experiences that I have and it's difficult for me to get along with them 100 percent. [For example] here in the Czech Republic we all grew up playing with just five types of toys – there just weren't more ... in this stupid socialist country. And these are the things we all share, these memories. We share the demons of our common past, the same hang-ups.«

What are the demons of my past and who shares them with me? Do we Bulgarians share our own unique demons? Unexpectedly, these questions seem to acquire an exceptional importance. In search of answers, I came across more surprises in Prague....

Der Tagesspiegel daily, Germany, 28 April 2004

A Smile at the Bus Stop (2004)

By Stefan Jacobs

Solange Olszewska once taught medicine in Berlin. Now she and her husband run a bus factory with 650 staff in Poland. The Berliner Verkehrsbetriebe (Berlin Municipal Transport Services) is one of their customers.

The Olszewski family's bus factory was previously a munitions factory and it looks like it: a clearing in the pine forest between poorly signposted villages near Poznan. An assembly hall and a bare concrete box crouch behind a rusty wire fence. Five busses are parked in front – looking as though they've landed from another planet: shiny, smooth, with tinted windows and a smiling designer front. They are painted blue and white – the colours of the Munich Municipal Transport Services, to which they will be handed over in a few days. The Poles have outdone Mercedes and the MAN Group.

The Poles? »I am a Berliner«, says Solange Olszewska, 53, who runs the company with her husband Krzysztof (»I only speak when my wife asks me!«). He runs operations in the main factory; his wife looks after sales and service from Berlin. Klaus Wowereit is happy to take her on his trips to Eastern Europe because she is a huge fan of Berlin as a location (»the best place in Europe if one wants to get involved«) and proves that not every Pole is a car thief or a peasant. Apart from that, Solange Olszewska is great at making long journeys pass quickly by telling her life story. It starts in 1981 when the motor mechanic Krzysztof Olszewski was buying used car parts in Germany and General Jaruzelski declared martial law in Poland. Krzysztof remained in Germany. His wife – a doctor – was able to follow him illegally. Their two babies had to stay behind with their gransmother in Poland. He obtained a job at the Neoplan bus factory in Spandau and she found a position at the Freie Universität. Her children were only allowed to leave thanks to a letter from the Foreign Minister Mr. Genscher.

Three years later, Krzysztof was head of the Neoplan factory in Spandau. Following the fall of the wall, he wanted to persuade the owners to expand into Poland where the Icarus buses would fall apart within a foreseeable period. In vain. They therefore agreed that he could move to the east at his own risk with a licence and try to sell his products there. In 1994, he sold his first bus in Warsaw; a year later he won a tender for 73 vehicles in Poznan, on the condition that the buses would be produced on the spot. With nothing but a delivery date in his hand, he coaxed a bank into giving him a loan and bought a ramshackle hall in the old munitions factory. The buses were ready on time. But they were not up to coping with Polish roads, as rapidly became apparent. »We therefore wanted to develop a bus for eastern Europe: modern, robust and smart«, says Solange Olszewska and smiles. She remembers December 1998 when the designers presented their prototypes and she immediately fell in love with their smiling faces. »Solaris« was written on the bus, which sounded like the sun and like her first name.

They soon had 70 orders in the bag. Their buses had a robust chassis and stainless steel parts to avoid damage from holes in the roads and the salt used in winter. While Neoplan stumbled and was taken over by the MAN Group, the Olszewskis managed to become the market leader in Poland and Latvia. Soon they were supplying companies in Switzerland. In 2000, the entrepreneur Richard Herrmann, who also drives for the Berlin Municipal Transport Services (BVG), bought his first two Solaris buses. »It was an East German who had the courage to do so«, says Solange Olszewska.

Now 16 Solaris buses are driving through Berlin in BVG colours; the next ones are on order. »Solaris« can be found on the inside but not on the outside – BVG refused to have the name on the front or the back.

In 2001, the Neoplan plant in Spandau was completed. The Olszewskis have 650 staff now. They want to build a second hall in their clearing soon because space is becoming tight.

Stefan Jacobs. *Born 1975 in Leipzig. Civilian service following secondary school. Vocational training as an optician, journalism school in Berlin. Following completion, he worked for the Berliner Tagesspiegel. Awarded the Young Journalist Prize of Saxony in 1995.*

Der Tagesspiegel, Germany, 30 April 2004

The Art of Saving a Palace (2004)

By Stefan Jacobs

Rundāle – For 40 years Imants Lancmanis has been trying to save Latvia's most sumptuous Baroque building from decay. He is making good progress but will never achieve his goal.

Rundāle Palace is like a Fata Morgana. In flat southern Latvia where greyish brown villages crouch between marshes, one turns off the country road to a handful of houses and sees a dazzling yellow and white Baroque façade of such dimensions that it makes Sanssouci Palace look like the gardeners' outbuildings. 138 rooms ranging in size from large to enormous surround the square that Tsarina Anna Ivanova constructed for her favourite, Ernst Johann von Biron, Duke of Courland from 1735. It provides a superabundant 7,000 square metres of living space, plus 70 hectares of courtyards and gardens.

Imants Lancmanis, a friendly man with a grey brush cut and aristocratic manners, has been living at Rundāle Palace for 40 years now. His grandiose office is situated on the second floor, just below the Baroque chimney on which a stork is just building his nest for his mate and a clutch of eggs. You can see him very clearly through the window if you follow the

»lord« of the castle through the labyrinth of corridors in the south wing. This is where Lancmanis' life's work is documented – even though he would consider this expression exaggerated. An exhibition explains the restoration of the palace, which Lancmanis has led for 32 years, and the completion of which he will not live to see. But he has come a long way. When he started in Soviet times, part of the palace was occupied by a boarding school – with basketball baskets beneath moulded ceilings. The majority of the rooms were empty. Many doors and windows were missing since they had been torn out and used as fuel in 1920. In the meantime, not only have the roof and heating system been repaired, but some 40 rooms have been restored to their original condition: silk wall coverings that were once purchased in Berlin and Potsdam have been newly woven in Moscow, oven tiles painted in the naïve style have been copied by artists from Saint Petersburg, mirrors with moulded frames have been repaired and parquet floors restored. A »Courland« dinner service from the royal porcelain manufacturer has also featured in the display cabinet since Klaus Wowereit presented it to the Latvian president on a visit. Much of the furniture in the castle was lost during a visit by Napoleon's troops in 1812. But not everything. Lancmanis stops in front of two chairs covered with blue velvet. »These are original. We found them in a church. They were completely wrecked. We gave the pastor two solid oak chairs in return«, says the director, smiles and adds, »a good exchange.«

Under the Soviets there were neither enough resources nor sensible colours for the façade. Now, as the 1980s yellow is flaking off again, everything is available except enough money. »The *nouveaux riches* Latvians will not spend money on something as beautiful as this but prefer to buy a Mercedes. Patronage of the arts needs to develop first.« The director understands that the state contributes hardly any money. »Pensions are more important.«

However, a British man recently gave 48,000 pounds, the great-great-great-great-great-great grandson of the builder paid for the restoration of the parquet floor in the duke's bedroom and the Russian Rolls Royce boss paid for the renovation of the duchess's apartments.

Lancmanis indicates a couple of wall paintings that have been painted over. »They must be uncovered using chemicals. It takes years and it is terribly expensive. Perhaps the EU will give something towards it.« Then he smiles again – more inwardly. It's not a businessman who is smiling, rather somebody who still has dreams.

Der Tagesspiegel, Germany, 27 April 2004

The Cellar that Gives You a Lift (2004)

By Stefan Jacobs

Gyöngyöspata – a Hungarian winegrower is boosting tourism.

The beautician had just popped in to collect a bowl of sediment from the wine barrels. She needs it for her homemade moisturiser, which she is first going to try on her relatives and then probably sell to her clients. Now that the beautician has gone, Magdi Bernáth has time. She lights a candle and opens the door to the cold, damp vaults beneath her house. The last 20 metres are blocked in places but in the front part there is still enough space for two dozen barrels and a few hundred bottles of wine. The landlady selects a bottle of red, polishes the bottle and uncorks it, sniffs the glass she has just filled and exhales. »If I spent half an hour here, I would not be tired any more.«

The house is two hundred years old and the front part of the cellar three hundred; for a long time nobody knew how old the rest was until two years ago Magdi Bernáth had it looked at by an expert, who dated one of the pointed stone arches to the 14th century. At the time, the cellar belonged to the church, which hoarded its tithes here. Subsequently people lived there; there is even still a cooking area from which you can catch a glimpse of the sky through a chimney.

When she bought the house in Gyöngyöspata 15 years ago, Magdi Bernáth was still the manager of a mineral water company. The 54-year-old was born in the village 80 kilometres east of Budapest. But before she penetrated deep into her cellar and the art of viticulture, she began to appreciate the thinly populated area on the southern slopes of the Mátra Mountains. She gave up her job and founded the »wine route«, a federation of 16 villages that wanted to attract tourists to the area, which was virtually unknown even to many Hungarians. The local administration provided some money for information boards and signs for hiking trails. Everything else is looked after by the local landlords and landladies, hoteliers and bakers – under the direction of Magdi Bernáth: they organise church concerts, cook for their guests, show them how the wine arrives in the bottles, and have established the old vicarage as a regional museum. People are not expecting mass tourism following Hungary's accession to the EU but they are enjoying their first successes: a Finnish group has just visited and was astonished by the beauty of the gently rolling countryside with its blossom-covered fruit trees and about the quality of the wine from the Mátra Mountains, of which they had never heard before.

Yesterday, after the Finns left, Magdi Bernáth uncorked the first bottle from the 2003 vintage, purely out of curiosity. Since then, she has looked forward to going into her cellar even more.

Deutschlandfunk radio, Germany, 14 June 2008

Faces of Europe: The new foreigners – Greece and its immigrants (WINNER 2008)

Reports from Anna Koktsidou

Presenter:
The outer borders of the European Union are borders of wealth. Here poverty encounters prosperity. The influx continues of those who spare no effort to turn their backs on the poverty in their own countries and come to Europe at any cost. As it is becoming increasingly difficult to legally pass into the stronghold of Europe, thousands and thousands try it illegally every year, running great risks each time. No-one knows how many people lose their lives in these dramatic escapes.

Vanishing point Southern Europe, Mediterranean location: In addition to Italy, Spain and Malta, Greece is developing into one of the main destination for refugees. They attempt to cross the borders by way of Turkey and the Eastern Mediterranean Sea to come to Samos, Lesbos or Chios. All of these Greek islands can be seen from the Turkish mainland. Greek authorities are overwhelmed and are increasingly faced with criticism. Last autumn, refugee organisations accused them of the systematic violation of human rights, scandalous assaults by the Greek coast guards, asylum rights that do not meet the requirements of international minimum standards, and unbearable conditions in the overcrowded refugee camps.

ATMO

Presenter:
Patras, in the southwest of Greece. The seaport at the Ionian Sea is called »Gate to Europe« and the boat-people from Afghanistan, who are stranded here, take this description literally. They try to survive in slums without water or electricity and they have no hope at all to be accepted as refugees or asylum seekers. All they want is to get away – and so they hope that Patras will be their gate to Northern Europe.

Report 1: Hardship for refugees in Patras: Unattainable hopes for a better life in Europe

ATMO

Author:
The harbour promenade in Patras. On one side the sea and the huge ferries, soon on their way to Italy. On the other side, fancy new apartment buildings with

a view of the waterfront and of the Afghan refugee camp adjacent to their property. There are about a hundred shabby huts with floors made of of wooden pallets, walls and roofs made of cardboard, and the entire construction covered with plastic,held together by cords and strings. At least they offer some shelter against the weather:

ATMO

Author:
Said is standing at the entry of the camp. He is 22 years old, short and slim. Said doesn't live in the camp. After having invested a lot of time and effort he has finally found a room in Patras. As an asylum seeker he was eligible for the so-called »Pink Card«, which allows him to work. Said occasionally finds a job at construction sites and helps the public authorities as an interpreter, thereby earning some money. Almost every day he shows up at the camp to translate. He knows everyone there and everyone knows him.

Original soundtrack: Said 1
They tap the electric wires illegally. So many people without electricity – that can't be possible. To get the electricity by tapping on the wires is dangerous. Once someone lost his life. But what should they do? The

authorities turn off the electricity again and again, but it goes on again, sometimes ten times a day, off and on, off and on....

Author:
The electricity is mainly needed to run TV sets and radios, sometimes even a refrigerator. Yet the cooking is almost always done on outside fireplaces.

Original soundtrack: Said 2
The water is stolen, too.... Back there in the ditch there are two hoses. They must be enough for all. Of course that's only cold water. Whoever wants to wash his dishes must line up, whoever wants to shower as well, and sometimes there are fierce fights about who is going to be first.

Author:
At the ditch a few men are washing food for their supper. A little further down someone is brushing his teeth. At times the smell of feces creeps into your nose. There are no sanitary facilities; bushes and the ditch serve as toilets. But, all in all, in spite of these humiliating circumstances, the men try to keep the camp as clean as possible.

ATMO

Author:
On one part of the property a larger hut is being constructed with wooden boards. A small group of Greeks teach refugees their language. But the majority of the inhabitants of Patras are disparaging and some are downright hostile.The immigrants are only welcome as illegal workers and only earn a minimum wage. Said complains that often they are treated like beggars.

Original soundtrack: Said 3
No one here takes care of the refugees. On TV every day they report only badly about the foreigners. The people in Patras are afraid of us refugees. As if we were not human beings. To prolong an exceptional permission to remain, you need an apartment, but nobody rents you one. As soon as the landlord knows we are Afghans, he says no.

ATMO

Author:
Said smiles wearily, his eyes glare, his skin is sallow. He has a slight fever, but instead of sitting in his room or going to the doctor he takes care of his fellow Afghans. Said has been living in Greece now for four years. Ever since his first day he has been fighting with the public authorities about his right to stay.

Original soundtrack Said 4:
I stayed here because I thought I could live here. To build something up. I was twelve when I went away from Afghanistan, I longed for a better life. By now I am tired. Sometimes I don´t want any more. For ten years I have been in transit. It is not good here, but to go would probably be even worse.

Author:
Currently, almost 900 Afghan males live in these huts, from twelve-year-old boys to 35-year-old men. They all had have long journeys, like 20-year-old Server, a slim tall young man with short hair carefully combed out of his face. He does his best to somehow preserve his dignity. Server left his country five years ago and arrived in Greece 20 months ago.

Original soundtrack: Server 1
I had to leave Afghanistan because there my life was in danger. Together with my family we went to Pakistan. From there I fled to Iran. But the Iranians are even more extremist. And so I travelled on. And then I came here. Today I doubt that this was the right decision. If I could move freely in Afghanistan I would go back.

Author:
Server managed to escape on a boat from the Turkish coast to the island of Samos. He doesn't want to

talk about all the horrible details. From Samos his journey continued to Athens and then to Patras. He feels like a captive here and leads the life of an illegal immigrant: always watchful, always on the run. And the police lurk everywhere. Whoever dares to go outside and has no ID is immediately arrested. At the end of January, the police tracked down the illegal immigrants and tried to evacuate the camp. Heavy protests followed : in their desperation the Afghans went into the streets, and were supported by local human rights groups.

Original soundtrack: Server 2
Most of the men are here because they have no papers. When they are caught they go to prison for three or four months, and on top of that they have to pay a 100 euro fine.

Author:
But it doesn't happen too often that someone is actually deported, anyway. Where would they send him? Instead, the refugees have to organize their own departure. But most of them remain in the country illegally. This is the Greek refugee policy. Server shakes his head.

It wears him out to have no perspective at all. At night the men from the camp sneak off to the harbour area, climb over the borderline, and attempt to hang on to the vans to get closer to the ferries. More often than not they are discovered and chased away, sometimes even arrested. Only a few succeed, mostly those who have money. Until the police raids started, Server also went to the harbour every day, but he had no luck he says. Now he longingly looks towards the sea, as if, somewhere beyond the horizon, there were a place that promises him a better life.

Original soundtrack: Server 3
I want to cross this sea, I want to reach the other side in another country of the European Union. In Greece there is no future for me. Here I have absolutely no chance for a better tomorrow. That is why I have to go away.

MUSIC

Presenter:
The European Union continuously rearms its outer borders and spends millions trying to fend off the refugees. But patrol boats, night sensing equipment and motion detectors alone will not suffice to bring the migration problem under control.

»The truth may be bitter, but it must be told«. This is the title of a report about the situation at the border between Greece and Turkey compiled by the Human Rights organisation Pro Asyl, the European

Council on Refugees and Exiles (ECRE), and a group of Greek advocates. In this report, serious accusations against the Greek coast guards are made. The authors tell of systematic violations against human rights. Refugees arriving by boat have been regularly held off, intimidated, and forced to turn back. Some have even been beaten, mistreated, thrown into the sea, or marooned on uninhabited islands. The report was based on testimonies of more than 100 eyewitnesses and other persons involved. The government in Athens announced that the allegations would be subject to investigation. To this day, the results are still not available.

Lit 1:
Refugeee M from Afghanistan, interviewed on 21 July, 2007 in Mitilini

We used a little inflatable boat. We started at about two o'clock in the morning. After six hours on the sea we finally reached the Greek coast. About 300 metres before reaching the island of Lesbos, the coast guards detected us. It was a fast, white boat. They circled us at high speed. The police threw ropes toward us and we were taken on board. We were tired, totally exhausted, and all we wanted to do was sleep. We lay down on the floor. The police yelled: »Don't sleep, sit!« They kicked us. Another ship was called. They treated us roughly when they brought us onto that ship. We pleaded: »We are human beings. Please help us.«

The ship took us back. They threw our boat in the water a little less than two kilometres away from the Turkish coast. After that we were forced back onto it. They made a small hole in the boat and gave us only one paddle. We paddled desperately to reach the shore. After not quite one hour we gave up. We thought we were going to die. The water was totally calm. After some time we fell asleep. Then a large ship came and saved us.

Presenter:
In May alone, 57 boat people were picked up off the coast of Samos, 95 off of Farmakonissi, 26 in Patmos, and 300 off the coast of Leros. The crossing is not only dangerous because of the waves and the wind, the boats also risk getting between the fronts of the archrivals Greece and Turkey. There are practically no international waters between the Turkish mainland and the Aegean islands. The sovereign territories of the two countries adjoin in the narrow straits. The Turkish and Greek patrol boats are careful not to get to the other side and possibly provoke incidents. But they attempt to push the refugee boats to the other side.

ATMO: Music from radio: Turkish song

Presenter:
The border between Turkey and Greece is just as dangerous, since entire sections are still mined. The minefields are marked as such, but hard to make out in the darkness. There have been more than 100 casualties in the past 10 years, according to data from the United Nations. But this does not seem to keep anybody away. Last year alone, 17,000 refugees were picked up at this border on the banks of the River Evros.

Report 2: Escaping over minefields: The border between Turkey and Greece near Evros.

Author:
Skarlatos Kyralanis can pick up Turkish radio programming especially well when he is out in his fields. Dilofos, his village, is located only 500 metres linear distance from the Turkish border, and his field borders directly the River Evros. On one side of the riverbank, the Turkish farmers take care of their farmland, on the other side it's the Greeks. In the mornings they greet each other with, »kalimera« or »merhaba«. At this point the river is not even one hundred metres wide and easy to cross – it is seemingly only a very small step to the European Union.

Original soundtrack: Farmer Kyranalis 1:
Sometimes they come over with a rubber boat. Sometimes one swims ahead with a rope, fastens it and pulls the others onto the riverbank. That happens mostly in the night. In the mornings I find abandoned boats or oars time and again. It also happens that they ask for help. I also have brought them to the police or to the military if they asked for it. That is the least I can do.

Author:
Skarlatos Kyralanis is in his early fifties, his face rosy from the work outdoors, his hair is beginning to thin out. He farms 20 hectares of land together with his 30-year-old son. Wheat, cotton, lentils, rape, tomatoes, sugar cane. This enables him not to be dependent on one harvest only. Skarlatos Kyralanis is a dedicated farmer, and, if need be, he will work around the clock.

Original soundtrack: Farmer Kyralanis 2:
Once I went into the field in the nighttime to water and because I wanted to see if everything was all right. All of a sudden I saw a black figure in the headlight of my car. I was so terrified – such a fear I have never had in my life before. A black man jumped away and disappeared. I went to the police but they couldn´t find him. The next day the fishermen got a corpse out of

the river. I don't know if it really was this man but he resembled him a lot.

Author:
The river is just not that easy to pass, says Kyralanis. Some refugees can't swim, some are ill or very weakened, others run into the minefields that the NATO partners Greece and Turkey have positioned on both sides of this border. The minefields are fenced in, and signs warn the trespassers about the danger. Nevertheless, there are refugees who cut the wire netting and enter this dangerous area. Once Kyralanis was an eyewitness to one of these incidents. He was extremely worried that the men might step on a deadly mine. But as if by a miracle they remained unscathed. Later he informed the military what had happened.

ATMO: Bulgarian radio programme

Author:
With a small twist of the radio dial, Kyralanis can listen to a Bulgarian radio programm. Bulgaria is only seven kilometres away and is increasingly turning into the new vanishing point, especially since this country has become a member of the EU. There always was illegal immigration at this border, but now it is increasing, Skarlatos Kyralanis believes.

Original soundtrack: Farmer Kyralanis 3

In autumn and in winter, a lot more people come than during the other seasons. Perhaps they work all summer to earn money for the passage. Well, they have to pay a whole lot for this. A Greek takes $2,000 to transport them from here to Athens. So you can imagine what the Turkish take to bring them from the border of Irak to Evros. That is still an enormous distance! If they come in winter it is cold and it rains. The waters in the river rise. But possibly they think they can cross unnoticed in these times. None of us are out in the winter. It is deserted here.

Author:

Kyralanis assumes that there are some people who profit by helping the refugees. He notices that the refugees always head in the same destination. Almost all of them have mobile phones and follow the instructions. But human traffickers are rarely caught. Those refugees that were picked up by the border patrol were forced to stay at the police stations, where the conditions were said to be difficult. There was not enough space and the police were afraid of diseases that the refugees might bring into the country. In the neighbourhood community there was a brand new reception centre – but would it be enough for all newcomers?

ATMO: Greek television

Author:
Kyralanis has arrived at home. The house in which he and his wife lives is big, too big for both of them. The older son runs a restaurant in Orestiada, the next district town. His younger son, who works with him on the fields, has a small apartment in Orestiada. These days only 300 people live in the village, most of them elderly. But it is not quiet here.

Original soundtrack: Farmer Kyralanis 4
Life here is hard. Our income varies every year. One time the harvest is good, another time it isn't. We are cut off from the outside world. At least the men are occupied all day on the fields and are distracted from the misery. But the women! They suffer. They are at home day and night. In the evenings I fall into bed while my wife lies awake and listens for someone knocking on the window. Sometimes we are really frightened. For example, when we hear that 20 people crossed the previous night. Here we seldom have good news. No births, no baptisms, no weddings. Only minefields and church services for the dead.

Author:
At the same time, Kyralanis has sympathy for those who have fled to come here – they come out of bare

needs, he says. Skarlatos Kyralanis knows what it means to go away and leave everything behind. He once tried his luck in Germany, like many others from his village who were unemployed. Kyralanis couldn't bear living in Germany.He had to return to his fields. But for the refugees there is no way back.

Original soundtrack: Farmer Kyralanis 5
We can't keep the people from coming. I think they would not try to escape if they were doing well at home.

MUSIC

Presenter:
As an EU member, Greece is exposed to harsh criticism concerning its refugee and asylum policy. The EU committee even took legal action against the Greek asylum policy at the European Court of Justice. The refugee aid organisation of the United Nations has called on the European states not to deport any more refugees to Greece. Nowhere else in Europe is the rate of acceptance as low as it is in Greece: 0.6 per cent.

Only very few states comply with the request. The others refer to the Dublin Agreement, which regulates the deportation of asylum seekers – namely, always back to the country where their first entry was registered.

This puts the member states at the outer borders of the EU at a disadvantage. Greece complains that it has to carry the burden alone. According to the government in Athens, the Dublin Agreement has to be revised, especially regarding European solidarity.

Lit 2:
Laaleh Z., Iranian, interviewed on 14 May, 2007
1.32

> *There were about 25 to 27 of us when we crossed the River Evros. We stepped onto Greek ground and were discoverd by uniformed men. They asked us to stand still and they shot in the air.*
>
> *We were pushed, even my little daughter. Nine from our group were arrested, the others escaped. We were brought into a prison where we spent two nights.*
>
> *The conditions in the prison where terrible. My child suffers from heart problems. We were at the mercy of the policemen. Our Palestinian fellow prisoners were beaten.*
>
> *On Tuesday, 20 March 2007, the police commanded us to get into a van at four in the morning. We were brought to the river. There were about 150 refugees from Irak, Somalia, Eritrea,*

Algeria, Iran, et cetera. In groups of 20 to 30 people, the police forced us to board a boat. We were brought to the opposite bank of the Evros, to the Turkish side.

The captain was a Greek. He went back and forth from one side of the river to the other. My little daughter and I were pushed into the water near the Turkish side, and the boat left.

Presenter:
In 1989 Greece became a destination for immigrants practically overnight. First the Eastern bloc collapsed, then Yugoslavia toppled.

ATMO

Presenter:
Then the Albanians started to come. To this day they constitute the largest group among the one-and-a-half million foreigners. The Albanian community in Greece numbers 600,000 people. Many try to benefit from the new immigration law. It gives them the possibiltiy to receive a residence permit, yet only if they can prove they have permanent employment and if they pay a certain fee. Many work under conditions under which others would never work, for example in Drama, a small town in the north.

Report 3: Homesickness in their hearts and sores on the palms of their hands: Albanians in the north of Greece

Author:
The cutting machine is several metres high and moves to and fro on rails. The workers put iron rods into the running engine. Then the rods are bundled and hauled onto trucks. Foreigners are not welcome on the site. The danger of having an accident is huge. But at the same time, those working at the site don't wear helmets or gloves.

Original soundtrack: Prepari 1

You can't wear gloves while doing this work. Last year I got caught here with my fingers. If the glove gets caught in the machine, you can't get your hand out any more. The helmet? Well, it hangs there in the corner. It's impractical, because you always have to put your head down and then lift it again. But, yeah, up to now nothing has happened.

Author:
Prepari Bekio is approximately 165 centimetres tall, slim and wiry. His skin is tanned, his face full of deep wrinkles, the traces of hard outdoor work. He is only 36, but he looks ten years older.

ATMO 1 work again high

Author:
Prepari is the only foreigner in the company. He earns 40 euros a day, about 800 per month. He is a day labourer like many others in Greece, both locals and immigrants. When the weather is bad you get no money. Prepari considers that all right; the boss does not earn anything himself on those days, he reckons. He gets along well with him, each can rely on the other. Above all, Prepari now has a social insurance and can thereby give proof of his working days, without which, in turn, he wouldn't get his annual residence permit.

Original sountrack Prepari 2
You need a lot of papers and one day isn't enough to get everything settled. For the residence permit, I have to verify 150 working days per year, and I have to pay 150 euros for one year and an additional150 euros for my wife.

ATMO 2 Baby – family

Author:
A couple of hours later Prepari – who has just taken a shower – is sitting with his family in the living room of his apartment. Four rooms, 110 square metres, third

floor, in an old building without an elevator in the city centre of Drama. While the Greeks move out to the green outskirts of the city where they are offered roomy one-family houses, more and more migrants move into the narrow alleys of the centre. Albanians, Ukrainians, Greeks from the former Soviet Union. Prepari's relatives – one of his brothers, several cousins, and their spouses and children – live just around the corner, The apartments here are affordable and the Bekios are content with what they have achieved so far.

Original soundtrack Prepari 3
In Albania there was no work, no money. For the work I do here I would have earned two to three euros a day. Should I have begged my father for something: give me money to buy cigarettes or to have a coffee with a friend?

My father had work until 1990. Now he is 62. If I didn't send him money he wouldn't even be able to afford a cup of coffee.

Author:
Prepari also sends money to other relatives. Only last year he funded the wedding of one of his sisters. In order to manage all this he also works illegally, as a painter, tiler, electrician, or gardener.

Prepari has been in Greece for ten years. Like all Albanians he crossed the border illegally. Of course it was dangerous, he says. On the way across the mountains they encountered bears and criminals, as well as the border police. Twice he was picked up by the Greek police and deported. The third time he made it all the way to the city of Drama where he had relatives. They provided him with jobs, first working for a shepherd and then at construction sites. Prepari tarred and hauled stones for the new highway that leads from Komotini in the east up to Thessaloniki in the west. Later he was lucky to find an employer who was willing to insure him. This enabled him to receive a residence permit and he could bring his wife in.

ATMO Baby

Author:
Feride came with the baby. Little Alexander was born in Greece, just like the middle child, eight-year-old Christina. In retrospective everything seems to have been so easy, she says, but when Prepari first came to Greece he didn´t even have money to call her.

Original soundtrack Feride
Nine months I didn't hear anything from him. From whom should I have heard anything anyway, from carrier pigeons? I was so worried.

In the beginning it was really hard for me here. I couldn't speak the language. I felt as if I were mute. People on the street would ask me what time it was and I could only hold out my watch to them.
Author:
But now all of them speak Greek, even 34-year-old Feride. They can now all communicate without any problems. Every now and then she earns some money as a cleaning lady in Greek households, but with the baby she has little spare time to do this.

ATMO Coffee cups

Author:
Prepari and Feride didn't plan on staying in Greece for good. But in the meantime they have entirely adjusted to their new home country and do everything to make their children feel as if they were not foreigners.

ATMO Antigoni and Baby

Author:
Antigoni, Prepari's eldest daughter, comes home. She has a Greek first name. That's a coincidence and in no way a sign of assimilation, her father says. The twelve-year-old just had her English lessons, and although she is one of the best in her class, she also takes private

lessons. Prepari remarks that he hopes one day his children will be better off than him and his wife, and proudly shows Antigoni's school reports. Effort and honesty are very important to him. He considers these two qualities to be the prerequisites for being successful and for reducing mistrust and prejudice.

Original soundtrack Prepari 4
We came because we were looking for work. We wanted to build a house and then return. But as things are developing I can't see us returning back home. The house in Albania is almost ready. But will we ever live there? Maybe once or twice a year when go back for a visit or perhaps some time later, when we have retired. But the children definitely won't go back. Their future lies here.

MUSIC

Lit 3:
Refugee A, Palestinian. Interviewed on 18 June, 2007 in Chios
When I was brought onto the coast guard boat, we were all immediately beaten. First I thought: We are free now, in Greece, in Europe, with its human rights and other advantages. But it didn't turn out to be that way. The officials beat the people.

When they realized that I spoke English, I was in trouble. First they grabbed me and thrashed me. Then they asked: »Where do you come from?« I said: »From Palestine.«

»And where did you start from?« »From Libya«, I said.

»On what ship – do you remember the colour, the name?« I said: »I can't remember what colour, what name.« »Okay«, they said, »you are lying«. Then they beat me. They brought a bucket and dunked my head into the water. »There, can you remember now?« they asked. »No, I don't remember.«

They brought me to the rear of the ship so that none of my friends could see me. Again and again they dunked my head into the bucket and asked: »You still don't remember?« I said: »Please don't hurt me, I only want freedom, I am longing for a good future, please help me!«

Presenter:
The refugee organisation Pro Asyl and the European Council on Refugees and Exiles (ECRE), which interviewed 100 people last year, report nearly identical complaints about harassment and mistreatment by the Greek coast guards. They call for complete clarification of all of the incidents on the Mediterranean Sea. They demand free access to fair asylum procedures, a ban on obligatory imprisonment, humane accommodation, and better protection for minors.

These are all violations to the Geneva Refugee Convention and they reveal political shortcomings. Although currently the coordinated common migration policy in the EU is still minimal, a conclusive concept for asylum, refugee and immigration policy in Greece does exist – even if the Greek government is at a loss regarding the migration phenomenon.

ATMO

Presenter:
This also applies to the integration policy. Only slowly has the insight grown that Greece has become a destination for immigrants. And debate on how to react to this has only started hesitantly. Conclusive answers are still missing. The many deficiencies must be remidied as soon as possible. For example there are still no publicly funded language courses. Immigrants have to rely on private initiatives organized by dedicated people to have a chance to learn the language.

Report 4: DIY language courses:
a private intitiative tries to respond to the government's shortcoming

ATMO 1: class

Author:
Cigarette in the left hand, pencil in the right – this is how Amalia stands in front of her pupils. A small, chubby woman in her early fifties, with short grey hair and round blue glasses. On the flipchart she writes Greek verbs: λούζω – λούζομαι ,- πλένω – πλένομαι, and explains the difference between »I wash« and »I wash myself«, and between »I wash« and »I wash the dishes« and »I clean«.

ATMO 1: high

Author:
In front of her there are ten men sitting at bistro tables arranged in a semicircle, from the eighteen-year-old to the fifty-year-old. All of them are either refugees waiting to hear about a decision regarding their asylum application, or migrant labourers who already have their papers. Among them are also two female students from Spain who have come to Athens for half a year.

ATMO 1: high again

Author:
Amalia doesn't use a schoolbook to teach. She selects the material according to the needs of the pupils as well as her own preferences. She choses poems and songs that are relevant to the topics she treats.

Original soundtrack Amalia 1
I assume that I deal with people who have little contact with the Greek language, and some of them may even be illiterate. For these people I have to find a different approach. We begin with vocabulary that is important for everyday communication, for example, words concerning the topic of work. This is truly a vital matter for most of my students. I want to open up a different window to Greece for them.

ATMO 2: CD louzetai i agapi mou...

Author:
The course takes place every Friday afternoon in the *Steki ton metanaston*, the »meeting-point of the migrants« in the Athenian quarter known as Exarchia, the quarter of the alternatives, intellectuals and anarchists. It is a small house in a narrow alley; the meeting-point is organized by different support

groups, and offers language and computer courses, discussion evenings and cultural events. Amalia's class takes place in the café. The walls are ochre, the window frames are auburn, the back room is green. The migrants who have come here from all over the globe are as diverse as the volunteers working here.

ATMO 3: singing of the group

Author:
After grammar lessons, part of a text is read out loud, and then everyone, including the 20-year-old Kurd from Syria, the 50-year-old Egyptian, and the students from Spain, joins in to sing a poem by Federico Garica Lorca, which was translated into Greek. For Amalia it's crucial that a couple of EU citizens are also taking part in the course. Therefore she asked for support from Beniat. The 26-year-old Basque is a music teacher. He accompanies the singers with his guitar, while Amalia stands in the corner and smokes her next cigarette. Beniat has been living in Athens for the past two years. He came because he had fallen in love with a Greek woman. And despite the fact that they had broken up before he moved to Athens, he moved anyway. As an EU citizen, he didn't have to worry about a visa, a residence or a work permit.

Original soundtrack Beniat

My journey was ever so simple. I got onto the airplane and that was it. However, many of those here had to cross the mountains by foot, swam across the sea or had to row, always risking their lives. As a music teacher I also benefit from the lessons, I learn many Greek songs and pick up some Kurdish and Bulgarian. But that's not all. As a migrant I feel the obligation to help. As citizens of this world we are all in charge.

ATMO 4 Music: second song

Author:

With an almost motherly glance Amalia looks at her group. The boyish woman in jeans and leather vest is highly respected by the men. She has taught them Greek dances and has gone to the theatre with them. If one of the men leaves his wife at home and comes alone, he is politely but firmly asked to leave. As an avowed feminist, she won't accept that. Again she lights a cigarette.

Amalia is a professional Spanish teacher. She earns her living by teaching language courses. She lived in Spain for a long time and was always committed to left-wing groups. She supported a school for Indians in Chiapas. But eventually she told herself: it can't be that I try to support the world, but when the world is standing at my front door, I'm not doing anything. This is when she started to give Greek lessons on a volunteer basis. That´s what she calls practising solidarity.

Original soundtrack Amalia 2
So whoever doesn't enjoy this should stay at home. I love what I'm doing. I love the boys. I am increasingly more able to understand their problems, I am a part of their world as they, in the meantime, have also become a part of our world.

Music

Lit 4:
Refugee A, Palestinian
»They took a plastic bag and put it over my head and choked me. I couldn't breathe anymore. They did that three times. I pleaded them to stop. ›Tell us the truth and we will let you go.‹ Then they took a gun. ›Do you see this gun?‹ they asked me. ›Yes, I see it!‹ ›Do you want me to kill you? Well, if you won't tell the truth....‹ Then they held the pistol against my temple and fired, directly over my head. All my friends thought I was dead.

I am not angry, but I want to tell the policemen: ›Please don't do anything like that to other people. They come here to live in peace. They have fled from their countries because of the war!‹«

Presenter:
Sealing off the borders, discouraging immigration, and deporting – Europe does not want to confine itself by only taking these measures against illegal migration. In the wake of the Tampere Summit in 1999, the main features of a common European migration and immigration policy are finally beginning to develop. A policy of »open gates« shall be reintroduced in the stronghold of Europe, the possibilities of legal immigration will be improved and broadened. The introduction of the »Blue Card« is one example. Seasonal work another. The EU wants to control migration as insight has grown within the European Union that it needs immigration.

The most recent suggestions aim at a common European agreement on immigration and asylum. The immigration and asylum policy is to be harmonized; the aim is to cooperate more closely with the countries from which immigrants come. In the future, development policy and migration policy should go hand in hand. Finally there is talk about a European integration treaty targeted towards promoting language, culture, and lifestyle in accordance with the principles of challenge and support.

ATMO

In the end, however, governments are unable to control people's everyday interaction with one another.

Tolerance and openness towards foreigners can't be forced. Migration is not a menace, but an enrichment. A theatre group in Athens tries to communicate this message: their play is called One Out of Ten, in reference to the fact that every tenth person in Greece is a foreigner. One Out of Ten became a hit of this year's theatre season.

Report 5: One Out of Ten, a play about the everyday life of migrants in foreign surroundings.

ATMO: The Internationale, part with the names...

Author:
The theatre Neos Kosmos in Athens. Three young men – an Albanian, a Georgian and a Bulgarian – are standing on stage. They are thinking about the past in their home countries and are narrating stories about their current life in Greece. Mareglen, Kostia and Ivan, who now call themselves Marios, Konstantinos and Jannis, gave themselves Greek names so the Greeks would accept them more easily. This desire for acceptance is the main theme in the play One Out of Ten. It is a desire well known to all migrants, says Kris, the Bulgarian, one of the three actors.

Original soundtrack Kris 1:
This is about all those who are forced to change their names so they would no longer be recognized as foreigners. But he who does that erases his past. And I don't believe that a person can be happy when he deletes his past from his life. Sometimes even employers demand that you change your name. This is also part of the play. It happened to me as well. I should have been called Christos although my name is Krastin. I refused to take on the name. Now I call myself Kris, I have simply shortened my name.

ATMO 2:

Author:
Kris is standing on the stage wearing a t-shirt, a spotlight on his athletic body accentuates his muscular arms. He talks about what it is like to be exploited by Greek employers or to be forced to prostitute oneself for a couple of euros, only because you need the money to bribe the authorities dealing with foreigners. In the beginning even men approached him on the street, Kris remembers, and he asks himself if they would have dared to approach him in the same way if he had been a Greek. When he jobbed as a pizza delivery boy he had to put up with being told that he, as a Bulgarian, should be especially nice and polite in order not to get into

trouble, and that he should under no circumstances mess around with the police.

Original soundtrack Kris 2

Initially when I came to Greece I was constantly under surveillance. One day, when I was walking along the street, there were two Pakistanis ahead of me, two Chinese behind me, and I, the Caucasian, was picked out by the policemen. »Hey guys,« I said, »why me, the Caucasian? Why not the others?« They took me to the police station and checked everything. After they had found out that I went to the drama school and was occupied with something decent, they were very nice. We even had coffee together.

On the other side of the street from my drama school is the Aliens Department. People stand in long queues waiting for their turn. The officials treat them like animals, jostle them and scream at them, »Go away! What do you want here?« And then the authorities make it clear that they would be prepared to give them a residence permit if they pay a huge amount of money.

ATMO 3 Theatre play: naturalization

Author:

Kris Radanof is 34 years old. He grew up in the town of Russe, near the border between Bulgaria and Rumania. He studied to be a nuclear technician, but has also worked as bodyguard and doorman – hence his athletic body. Seven years ago, after losing his job, he joined his mother in Athens. She had already lived here for a while and worked as a beauty specialist. In Greece, Kris decided to fulfill his childhood dream of becoming an actor. He worked hard to reach this goal; »as someone who has grew up in a socialist country, I know all about discipline«, he joked, his blue eyes sparkling. Kris went to drama class and has already celebrated his first successes both in the cinema and on TV. Ironically, he starred in the role of a foreigner.

Original soundtrack Kris 3
On screen I find it normal to play a foreigner. My physiognomy is that of a foreigner, and screen roles obviously depend on what you look like. But I want to work hard on my pronounciation, until no one will notice any difference between me and a native speaker. Then I might be able to get other roles to play.

But to all those who ask me if I mind playing a foreigner, I always reply that the Greek actor must feel disadvantaged. I, in contrast, have already been a Russian, a Bulgarian, and a Macedonian, and had to work myself into every identity. Which one of us is more lucky? (laughs)

ATMO 4 Instrumental

Author:
When Kris was offered a role in the play One Out of Ten, together with the Georgian David Maltese and the Albanian Enke Fesolari, he didn't hesitate one second. The play is based on an idea by the Greek director Laertis Vassiliou, who originally comes from the Greek minority in Albania. Authentic stories are brought onto the stage, the experiences of the four artists and those of their friends and acquaintances. Kris put a lot of effort into this role.

Original soundtrack Kris 4
The play is a slap in the face of the Greeks. But actually we have taken out some of the really nasty parts. The director didn't want to pillory the Greeks. But of course we wanted to show their bigotry when they say things like, »I, I am no way a racist, but – it would be better if you foreigners went home.« (laughs)

ATMO 6 To vo´fà lámericano

Author:
The huge success of the play surprised him. The group has to plan additional performances, and even Amnesty International asked them to perform. The ensemble is proud of this. But most of all Kris remembers a performance they had for a school class:

Original soundtrack Kris 5
Those were students who had to retake exams and who blamed their own unemployment on foreigners. We were curious how the evening would go, and we were prepared to have tomatoes thrown at us instead of hearing applause. But instead they laughed and cried with us, and after the performance a young woman even said: »Until yesterday I was proud to be a racist, but now I have to apologize for that.« We were speechless.

ATMO 6 end applause

MUSIC

Presenter:
And that was Faces of Europe: The new foreigners – Greece and its immigrants. With reports by Anna Koktsidou. The statements by the refugees were read by Kerstin Fischer and Simon Roden. The music was selected by Babette Michel. And on the microphone Thilo Kößler says good-bye.

***Anna Koktsidou**, born in Northern Greece in 1962; 1970 migration to Germany; secondary school education in Stuttgart; university education in German language, literature and pedagogy in Tuebingen. Training as a journalist (internship) at Sueddeutscher*

Rundfunk (SDR). Since 1992 freelance radio journalist for Suedwestrundfunk, for ten years as news and politics editor; and specialized in migration topics for the past five years. Freelance journalist for Deutschlandfunk and Hessischer Rundfunk (migration topics), presentation and concepts for round table discussions about migration for NGOs, ministries and social organisations.

Radio Slovenia 2 Val 202, Slovenia, 11 February, 2004, 11:59

Slovakia or Slovenia? (2004)

By Tadej Kosmrlj and Mirko Stular

Introduction of the programme in the form of news JINGLE. »At the heart of Europe. A Europe of people with stories and stories without borders. In the programme ›Mitten in Europa‹ on Radio Val 202, Wednesdays at 12 o'clock«

Jingle: Radio Slovakia: »Radio Slovensko!«

News reader, Radio Slovenia: »An information programme from Radio Žurnal follows.«

Jingle in Slovakian: »Radio Žurnal slovenskeho roshlasu.«

Newsreader, Radio Slovenia: »During his last visit to his Slovenian colleague Anton Rop, the Slovakian Prime Minister Mikulaš Dzurinda was so taken by Rop's name (which means ›robbery‹ in Slovenian) that he lent him the notorious doctor Vražda to go skiing in the Tatra Mountains.«

Slovenian foreign language assistant: »The Slovakian word ›vražda‹ means ›murder‹ in Slovenian.«

Jingle in Slovakian: »Počuvate radio Žurnal.«

Newsreader, Radio Slovenia: »The Prime Ministers of Slovenia and Slovakia, Mr. Rop and Mr. Dzurinda, decided at the end of the official visit to ask the US president to publicly confuse the two countries again. Slovenian foreign language assistant: Republika Slovenija, Slovenska Republika (Republic of Slovenia, Slovakian Republic).

Newsreader, Radio Slovenia: »The two countries had too little publicity in the long run.«

Jingle in Slovakian: »Počuvate radio Žurnal.«

Newsreader, Radio Slovenia: »Fans of Slovakian beer from Ljubljana, including our Slovenian correspondent, have assembled today to protest against the constant rise of beer prices in Slovakia. Apparently prices have increased fourteenfold in the last twenty years.«

Slovenian entrepreneur from Bratislava: »Then a beer cost 2.5 korunas, today it costs between 20 and 30 korunas.«

Newsreader, Radio Slovenia: »If prices continue to rise, fans of Slovakian beer are threatening to block the route between Ljubljana and Bratislava.«

Extract from a Slovakian song: »U vazduhu škandal visi.« (There's a scandal in the air)

Newsreader, Radio Slovenia: A scandal is also looming in the imminent Group B ice hockey championship. Namely a Slovakian hockey star says:

Slovakian hockey player in Slovenia: »Slovenski hokejisti su najlepši hrači« meaning that the Slovaks are the best players. (But unfortunately in Slovenian »najlepši« means »the most beautiful«)

Jingle for the weather report:

Slovakian newsreader: »U tom totižnji boli na Slovenskom visoke toploti oko 15 stupina Celzija, a fukal toplji veter.«

Moderator: »Temperatures have risen considerably in recent days: a warm wind is blowing. The snow has melted virtually everywhere.

»And now the readings at 11 o'clock: Bratislava 2 degrees, north west wind 5 m/s, Košice 2 degrees, south west wind 2 m/s, Žilina 0 degrees, south west wind 3 m/s and Stropkov 1 degree, no wind.«

Traffic jingle in Slovakian: (Dopravni servis Radia Slovensko, honking – traffic noise)

Newsreader, Radio Slovenia: »No traffic problems are reported on the roads in Slovenia and Slovakia.«

Jingle in Slovakian: (Radio Slovensko)

Moderator: »A hot report from Slovenia! Staff on the second programme of the Slovenian state-owned radio Val 202 have confused Slovenia with Slovakia in a broadcast!«

Jingle for the programme »At the Heart of Europe« in Slovenian.

(End of the news)

SLOVAKIAN SONG

Moderator: »Following this hot report from Slovakia on confusing the two countries, a little cooling Slovakian music is advisable. Today we shall certainly not confuse Slovenia and Slovakia any more but clarify the terms as much as that is possible. We were mixed up often enough anyway.«

INSTRUMENTAL MUSIC: MUSIC: CAN'T TOUCH THIS – Slovakian (pirate copy, cut 3, ca. 0.40)

Passer-by in Bratislava: »In the two months I worked in Germany, everybody thought that I was from Slovenia and not from Slovakia. I was really upset that the Germans didn't know where Slovakia is, when it's much closer to Germany than Slovenia.«

Moderator: »Let's add the experience of the Slovenian student Mitja Rijavec, who is studying Slovakian and English in Nitra, to the experiences of the Slovakian student from Bratislava.«

Slovenian student in Nitra: »The Slovaks are also often mixed up, which they don't like, of course. The Slovaks even feel that Slovenia is better known than Slovakia. I cannot confirm that. Of course you react sensitively to something like that. Ultimately national feelings are something very personal. And this is why some people feel aggrieved if they arrive in a country and nobody knows where they are from.«

Moderator: »And here a story about the proverbially reliable French post ... Georges Vassal, a member of staff on the international programme on Slovakian radio.«

French journalist: »Two of my friends in France wrote me a letter. It was addressed ›Bratislava, Slovakia‹ . This letter first landed at the other end of France and then came by mysterious channels first to Ljubljana until it finally reached me after a considerable time in Bratislava. I realised that the French post, which was reputed for a long time to know something of geography, had completely overlooked the fact that Slovenia and Slovakia are not the same country.«

Moderator: »We've already been confused with Pennsylvania«, remembers Ada Filip Slivnik, the

Republic of Slovenia's ambassador to Slovakia. »But the most famous mix-up naturally occurred with President Bush.«

Slovenian ambassador to Slovakia: »I think that since then many Americans and Europeans know that they are two different countries. Seen in these terms, this mix-up was to some extent an advertisement.«

Moderator: »The solution is therefore obvious. If we run out of advertising ideas, the two countries only need to ask a global politician to mix up them publicly, for example, with the statement »I really liked the Slovakian coast (said with irony).«

We are of course interested in finding out whether Slovenia tends to be mixed up with Slovakia or Slovakia with Slovenia. Are we better known than they are?«

Slovenian ambassador to Slovakia: »The Slovaks already think that they are more often confused with the Slovenes than vice versa. In the past people almost always thought they were Slovenes. But since Slovakia has been making an effort to become better known, the average European or American no longer seems to have a clue. I think the fundamental problem lies in the fact that their names are so similar. Both have the same linguistic root ›Sloven -‹ in their respective national language. If you ask Slovaks where they are from, most do not use the international word ›Slovakia‹ but ›Slovensko’. I think that the Slovenes work harder at differentiating themselves. I also think that Slovakia suffers less from being less well known.«

Journalist: »You have certainly come across a lot of mix-ups even during your time in Bratislava. Some are unusual, to put it mildly.«

Ambassador: »I have not experienced it here in Slovakia. If people were to confuse Slovenia and Slovakia here, that really would be too much. But I have experienced it in Russia, in America and elsewhere. The Austrians, similarly, complain about being constantly confused with Australians.«

Journalist: »Do you see an opportunity for doing something jointly about it?«

Ambassador: »It would be interesting perhaps if the two countries tried to present themselves jointly. There are actually many similarities. Many Slovenes, for example, recognise their own country in most Slovakian tourist brochures or television spots. Beautiful mountains, lakes, old castles and karst grottos, all the things that Slovenia uses in its advertising. Perhaps Slovakia should also emphasise its specialities more, such as Liptauer.

Very few people know that this curd-based spread comes from Slovakia. On the other hand, Slovenia has the sea, the Lipizzaner horses ... everything that you don't have here in Slovakia.«

Journalist: »They also have Lipizzaner horses. Is that a problem?«

Ambassador: »That's true, but only Slovenia has Lipica.« (laughs)

INSTRUMENTAL

Moderator: »So Slovakia is two and a half times the size of Slovenia and has five and a half million inhabitants. Luboš Kačírek has been studying and doing research for four months in Ljubljana. Slovaks like this are rare.«

A Slovak student studying Slovenian: »What strikes me about Slovenia? Mount Triglav. A colleague said to me: ›If you go to Slovenia, then you must see a real country wedding.‹ I didn't know what that is. And I think that the ›country wedding‹ in this form no longer exists. Or does it? I became friendly with a Czech in Slovenia and we wanted to climb Mount Triglav together. It was June and the paths were still closed. A Slovene who has never climbed Mount Triglav, is not a real Slovene. But I have never climbed Mount Gerlach, the highest mountain in Slovakia.«

Moderator: »So virtually no Slovak is a Slovene although they call themselves Slôvenci (and that means Slovene in Slovenian). Not even Luboš, who is now working as an assistant in the historical institute of the faculty of education in Bratislava is a real Slovene. But the first passer-by whom we addressed on the street in Bratislava talked about Slovenia like an expert.«

Passers-by in Bratislava: »Slovenia is the first ex-Yugoslav republic that achieved independence. Slovenia is situated on the Adriatic and borders Croatia and Austria. We Slovakians also like to visit your country because it has glorious scenery that slopes beautifully into the Adriatic. I must admit that I have never been to Ljubljana but I have been to Piran, Portorož and also to Koper.«
»I only know where the country is. It has good athletes and beautiful scenery. We travel through Slovenia and Ljubljana to the Croatian coast.«
»An ex-Yugoslav Republic. I think it borders Italy and Austria. Your national coat of arms is similar to ours – it also has three hills and the colours on the flag are also blue, white and red. Slovenia has two million inhabitants, mountains and the sea.«

Jingle for the programme »At the Heart of Europe«
Slovakian student Luboš, who is studying Slov-

enian: »When I travelled to Slovenia for the first time, people told me that the Slovenes were as cold as the Germans. But I didn't feel like that. They are very nice and friendly.«

Moderator: »Our colleague from Slovakian radio with whom we chatted neither in slovénsko (Slovenian) nor in slôvensko (Slovakian) is also nice.«
Slovakian journalist Zuzana Borovska: »Oui. Zuzana Borovska.«
Moderator: »Bonjour, Zuzana.«
Zuzana: »Bonjour. Dober dan.«
Moderator: »Dobri den.«
Zuzana: »My experience is that the Slovaks admire the Slovenes greatly. We admire your economy, which is far better than ours.«

Moderator: Borut Meršak also has firsthand experience of the two countries' economic collaboration. He is the managing director of the Slovenian company Kovintrade in Bratislava.

Borut Meršak: »Economic collaboration between Slovenia and Slovakia is becoming more and more significant. However, it should be emphasised that there was a certain amount of distrust at the beginning, particularly on the Slovenian side. The Slovenians viewed Slovakia as an ex-socialist country without any quality goods. However, in the past ten years, we Slovenian businessmen have recognised that the Slovaks are well able to manufacture high quality products.«

Moderator: »Do Slovenian businessmen today have confidence in this market and this collaboration?

Borut Meršak: »Definitely. If you once win the Slovaks over, they remain friends for life.«

Moderator: »How has EU accession changed things?«

Borut Meršak: »Not much. Competition will increase with accession, but not to excess.«

MUSIC – Elan – SLOVAKIA

Moderator: A street that has borne the name of one of the greatest Slovenians for eighty years has been a feature of the Bratislava cityscape for even longer than the most popular Slovakian pop group Elán has been a feature of the music scene.

Inhabitant of Prešeren Street in Bratislava: »There is a plaque with details of this famous Slovene at the beginning of the street. Among other things he wrote the words of the Slovenian national anthem. Without doubt he's an important person for you. Prešeren Street is one of the oldest streets in Bratislava, but only a few people know it because it is so short.«

Moderator: »An inhabitant of Prešeren Street in Bratislava says this on the Slovenian cultural holiday (8 February), Prešeren Memorial Day, of all days.

»The Slovaks don't just have a street that is named after him, they can even read the works of Prešeren in their own language – one of the few peoples in Europe to be able to do so. Prešeren was translated into Slovakian by Lubomir Feldek.«

Slovakian translator of Prešeren: »Prešeren was the first Slovenian poet of whom I had heard – on holiday on the Slovenian coast in fact. At the time I still smoked. His verses about beautiful girls and the beautiful ›Urška‹ were printed on the cigarette packs. I think they are from the ›Nickelmann‹. Those are the first Prešeren verses that I read. I admired the fact that the Slovenians love their poet so much. Each time they light a cigarette they read his poetry. If only other peoples venerated their poets as much: the French Baudelaire, the English Shakespeare ... but no, only the Slovenes are that proud of their Prešeren.«

Moderator: »The translator of Prešeren, Feldek, has become a very well known personality in Slovakia. Many people recognise him on the street. Which Slovakian poet would they print on cigarette packets in Slovakia?«

Slovakian translator of Prešeren: »(Laughs ...) »I'd put it like this. Slovakia is a land of poets just as much as Slovenia. Following the end of the Great Moravian Empire, there was no written tradition, only an oral tradition in Slovakia for 500 years. This produced a rich popular poetry. Both countries have a very rich culture. They have many poets and prose writers including one or more ›Prešeren‹. Jan Botto, the author of the famous opic ›Janošik's Death‹, is a great Slovakian poet. His poetry could easily be printed on cigarette packets.«

Moderator: »The intellectual Lubomir Feldek goes on to say that the ›Slovakian Prešeren‹ is named Hviezdoslav. Of course a street has also been named after him in Bratislava.«

Jingle for the programme »At the heart of Europe«

Moderator: »If they have a certain feel for language, they can probably understand Slovakian more easily than Prešeren's poetry. We have reached the main reason for confusing the two countries. A glimpse at the passports for the two countries is a surprise for many: Republika Slovenija and Slovenska Republika.«

Slovakian professor of Slovenian in Nitra: »The Slovenian and Slovakian languages are very similar. I would say that the Czech language is most similar to Slovakian. From a historical viewpoint, they are both members of the Czech-Slovak linguistic group, that is the western Slavonic languages. But Slovenian (which is a southern Slavonic language) is also very similar to Slovakian. And this superficial similarity is sometimes a major problem for translators.«

Moderator: »Juraj Vanko is a professor at the Slovakian institute of the philosophy faculty in Nitra. But he worked for three years as a foreign language assistant at the university in Ljubljana. He has listed the words that are the same in both languages in a book and found a total of around 1,200.«

INSTRUMENTAL

Moderator: »Why does the word ›otrok‹ mean ›slave‹ in Slovakian today but ›child‹ in Slovenian? The ways in which languages evolve are sometimes unfathomable. Each language evolves in its own way even if its starting point was roughly the same. Let me simplify it: neither ›slaves‹ nor ›children‹ have the right to vote. In Slovakian the word acquired a different meaning over the centuries than in Slovenian.

»Words known as ›false friends‹ sound the same in Slovenian and in Slovakian but have different meanings. They are the cause of a great deal of misunderstanding.«

Slovenian foreign language assistant in Bratislava: »So Slovenian and Slovakian are very similar languages but at the same time they are very different. I always like to use the word ›stol‹, which means ›chair‹ in Slovenian and ›table‹ in Slovakian, as an example. We call a chair ›stolička‹. So what is a chair for a Slovene is a table for us. Or let us take the word ›drevo‹. For the Slovenes that means ›tree‹ and for us it means ›wood‹. Wood is called ›les‹ by the Slovenes. In turn, this word ›les‹ means ›forest‹ in Slovakian. When I write that on the board, my students come close to despair.«

Moderator: »But words like this are more often grounds for laughter. Let us stick with the word ›otrok‹ for a moment, which, as we have said, means child in Slovenian and slave in Slovakian. The Slovaks probably find it absolutely hilarious that we use stickers to draw attention to the fact that we have an ›otrok‹ in the car with us.«

Student of Slovenian in Bratislava: »When I came to Slovenia for the first time, I wanted to say that the wind is blowing. In Slovakian one says, ›Veter fuka‹. But ›fukati‹ in Slovenian does not mean ›blow‹, as it does in Slovakian, but ›shag‹. Of course all the Slovenes laughed their socks off.«

Moderator: »Olga Ružičkova is a student of Slovenian in Bratislava. Her professor is the foreign language assistant Saša Pokláč from the philosophy faculty in Ljubljana.«

Live telephone conversation: Hello, Saša, welcome to the programme. Greetings or »Ahoj« from Bratislava. *Ahoj. You have been working as a foreign language assistant in Bratislava for one and a half years. The summer term has just started. I think you had your first class yesterday.* Yes, I had my first class yesterday at 7:20 a.m. *Who comes to your classes, and why, if I may ask?* A system of credits was recently introduced at the university. This means that we no longer have traditional students, particularly linguists. Today, historians, ethnologists, journalists, biologists, sports students, in other words a very heterogeneous group, study Slovenian. *Why are they learning Slovenian? That's an interesting question. Do they want to work in Slovenia or what?* Of course. Primarily they want to pass exams for their degrees. A few know Slovenia from holidays, others want to apply for a grant and continue their studies in Slovenia. *Do your students find Slovenian difficult? What do they have the most problems with?* At the beginning they find pronunciation very difficult. *Last week when Tadej and I were in Bratislava, the weather was very good. It was warm, around 18 degrees. What's the weather like today?* This southern weather is over, winter has returned. This morning it snowed. *As we reported at the beginning of the programme, I hope your classes go well in Bratislava and that you enjoy yourself, Saša. I hope that we will see each other again in Slovenia soon.* Give my best wishes to the homeland.

Jingle for the programme »At the Heart of Europe«

Moderator: »Incidentally, there is another peculiarity in Slovenian with which the Slovaks have difficulty. Even language professors have problems with the dual grammatical number.«

Professor of Slavonic languages in Slovakia: »One of the greatest problems is the dual grammatical number, which does not exist in Slovakian. Other difficulties crop up with declination.«

Moderator: »Was the dual a problem for you?«

Professor: »Yes, and it is still a problem. But it helps when I chat a great deal in Slovenian, for example with my friends from Slovenia – the Strajner family, to whom I would like to send my best wishes at this point. Stane corrects me constantly. He always used the dual when talking about his wife and himself, and I can learn something from that.« (Laughs)

Journalist: »So ›we two‹ are now ending the conversation?«

Professor: »Yes, ›we two‹ are ending it, not ›we‹.« (Laughs)

Moderator: »Professor Juraj Vanjko from the university in Nitra on the linguistic gymnastics between Slovenian and Slovakian.

»From linguistic to physical gymnastics. The Slovaks only have one royal discipline, as Georges Vassal knows.«

French journalist in Bratislava: »The undisputed royal discipline in Slovakian sport is ice hockey, although there are fewer registered ice hockey players than footballers in Slovakia. It's easier to set up the infrastructure for football and also it's an easier game needing less equipment. Everybody here is proud of their hockey team. The Slovaks have a lot of successful players in the NHL and a lot also play in Finland, Russia and the Czech Republic. They are the real idols of the Slovakian public.«

Moderator: »The ice hockey player from the Slavija club in Zalog, Peter Gallo, has also found parallels between Slovenia and Slovakia in ice hockey.«

Slovakian ice hockey player in Slovenia: »We have more clubs than their players. We have 20 top teams while they have a total of five or six. We have 200 top players, they have 50 good ones. Ice hockey is our top sport.«

Moderator: »This is how gently the Slovakian ice hockey player deals with Slovenian ice hockey ... But the Slovenes and the Slovaks have one important thing in common with ice hockey as with other sporting disciplines: one opponent that simply has to be beaten. With us it's the Croats, with the Slovaks, it's the Czechs.«

French journalist in Bratislava: »The opponent that always gets the adrenalin flowing is the Czech Republic, particularly with ice hockey. It's a duel between two giants. The Czechs always have to be beaten, even in friendly matches.«

Moderator: »But in the few years of independence a far fiercer rivalry has emerged between us and the Croats than between the Czechs and the Slovaks. Perhaps because Slovakia only became independent one and a half years after Slovenia – on 1 January, 1993.«

INSTRUMENTAL

Moderator: »The question that was set last week in the competition on our web page, www.rtvslo.si/val202, asks: ›How many Slovakian ice hockey players play in Slovenian clubs?‹ The winner was – actually no one. Nobody knew the correct answer: four. To make matters worse we have a Slovakian sports doctor and a hockey trainer working for us.

»Today there is a new question for all those

who are interested in Malta or kynology. You can also contact us through our email address, sredievrope@rtvslo.si, with any other comments or questions.«

INSTRUMENTAL

Moderator: »Almost everybody – whether Slovaks or Slovenes with whom we came into contact a couple of days ago in Slovakia – and there were a lot of them – knows Andrej Rozman, professor of Slovakian at the philosophy faculty in Ljubljana.«

Professor of Slovakian in Ljubljana: »Slovakia did not fall within Slovenia's sphere of influence for a long time. But it is not true that the Slovenes were not concerned with Slovakia. Up until 1948 (the year of the communist seizure of power in Czechoslovakia, and of the break between Yugoslavia and the Soviet Union), and also subsequently, there were many Slovenes who were closely associated with Slovak culture. Unfortunately, this generation died out in the 1970s and 1980s. However, subsequent developments and the division of Europe into blocs prevented closer collaboration with Slovakia, and this is why the Slovenes orientated themselves towards the West. Plus, even before this, the Slovenes were traditionally closer to the Czechs than the Slovaks.«

Moderator: »People who are better informed also think about the question of the Roma in connection with Slovakia. Officially there are 200,000 Roma living in Slovakia, unofficially there are half a million. The differences within the ethnic group could not be greater. Norbert Šarkezy, a musician with a university degree, whom we met working in a restaurant in Bratislava, is no average Romany. Šarkezy believes that the Roma question will remain unresolved for a long time. Unfortunately, stories like the following one are still the norm, Svetlana Luhova«

Employee at the Slovenian embassy in Bratislava: »I heard that in a village in the east of the country people tempted children into school with bread. Because bread was distributed in the breaks suddenly virtually everybody came to lessons.«

INSTRUMENTAL

Moderator: »For many Slovenes, Slovakia is still subordinate to the Czech Republic in an ironic sense. Or we say something along the lines of: ›Look at this Slovak!‹« (In Slovenian, the word ›Czech‹ is used as a swear word.)

Professor of Slovakian in Ljubljana: »I don't think we have any stereotypes connected with the Slovaks. In the 15th century, the majority of Slovaks were peddlers and tinkers but we don't have any stereotypes. Various myths are also widespread in Slovakia. Perhaps that is why there are no stereotypes because contacts between us were rare and we did not have any political, economic or cultural disputes with each other.«

Moderator: »Professor Andrej Rozman will get to know those who start their degree course, their degree in Slovakian language and literature, in the autumn. It is being introduced for the first time this year at the Institute of Slavonic Languages in addition to courses in Czech and Polish.«

Professor of Slovakian in Ljubljana:

»I hope that these courses will be successful. They will add a new dimension to our culture. There are now four Slavonic peoples in the EU and it is important for us to work together within the Community and to build a bridge to those Slavs who are outside the Union.«

Moderator: »Just something to end with: The University is having an open day this weekend.«

Moderator: »For those who prefer to look at an issue in practical terms, something else: there is certainly a stereotype for a Slovakian woman. Many men agree that she has long legs, is attractive, perhaps a little shy....«

Slovenian student in Slovakia: »I don't know if that is a cliché or the result of observation.«

Moderator: »Another little tip for our male listeners, or rather a warning. Never tell a Slovakian lady that she is a ›lepa ženska‹ (beautiful lady). Don't be surprised! The problem is not with the word ›lepa‹ (beautiful)! All women are flattered by that. The problem lies with the word ›ženska‹, which does not mean lady in Slovakian as it does in Slovenian but woman or something more derisive.«

A Slovakian journalist reads a Slovenian text with a very strong Slovakian accent: »Dear listeners, this brings the programme ›Mitten in Europa‹ by Tadej Košmilj and Mirko Štular to an end. Best wishes also from Zuzana Borovska from Bratislava. (She tries to pronounce the first name correctly) Todej kaš ... koš ... mrlj. Tadej Košmrlj.«

Die Presse daily newspaper, The world behind Vienna, Austria, October 2006 to September 2007

The World behind Vienna – A Series on Central Europe (WINNER 2007)

By Martin Leidenfrost / Translation by Adrian Garcia-Landa and Marie Hofmann

THE WORLD BEHIND VIENNA is a series of portraits published throughout a year, each written in the style of a personal essay. The subject of the series is the area of Central Europe situated between the Alps and the Carpathians, somewhere around the cities of Vienna and Bratislava, Györ and Brno.

The stories told are from an area separated between four countries, four official languages and a score of ethnic communities, and yet everything lies just around the corner. The region has been called several names such as »Centrope«, but there are few inhabitants who view this border-dense corner of Europe as a single entity.

Wagon Slovakia

Every evening, a restaurant car goes from Vienna to Bratislava. Years passed until I discovered it, as this rolling gem is attached to a useless train. 21:50 Vienna West, 23:30 Bratislava main station: Whoever is in his right mind avoids this most laborious of train connections. It is almost a ghost train.

The restaurant car is run by a company that has always been an enigma to me. In the smoothly buzzing economy of the Slovak Republic, »Wagon Slovakia« is a wondrous exception: they serve warm Coke and cold red wine, and the entire energy of the personnel goes into verbose justifications, never into the removal of the numerous shortcomings. On the other hand, there is no cheaper restaurant car in the whole of Europe.

The fact that Wagon Slovakia serves the Vienna-Bratislava line made me enthusiastic. I immediately took it three times.

The first time I got in on an untypical evening, a holiday. I got myself a red wine, took a seat in the halfcircular, well-padded lounge, and tried to get the wine to drinking temperature with my hands. I was the only guest. The grey-haired waiter-cook was sitting around listlessly. In front of him was a pile of soon to be outdated timetables. The melancholy of the evening found its climax when the waiter-cook took a timetable and folded it into a paper airplane, but preserved his sense of duty by not launching it.

The second time was livelier. A handful of Slovakian Gypsies were drinking moderately in the middle of the wagon. On the opposite window-front, sitting on one of the six bar stools, was a young Austrian railway employee travelling to his company flat. Lost in thought, he observed the cheerful assembly with a mild smile. With the experience of a great traveller he managed to absorb two beers until Bruck an der Leitha where he got off. At the Petržalka station, the Gypsies made their exit.

From that moment on, the blond waiter-cook tried discreetly to get me out of the wagon, but I didn't understand his signals. Finally he showed me his little foam mattress and explained that he would have to get up at five. He sleeps on the floor of the restaurant car. Embarassed, I retreated into the next wagon that was totally empty.

On the third journey, Wagon Slovakia gave me the full show. Exactly the same guests were assembled, on exactly the same seats. The railway employee had already got hold of his first goodnight beer, the Gypsies were drinking champagne, and we observed them with a mild smile.

The personnel had doubled, but this time the grey-haired waiter was in a better mood and the blond waiter had already had a few. On the little crisps-trolley, his small cassette player blared Bódi Gusztí, a furious Hungarian Gypsy band. The waiter had opened his shirt widely and got into such rapture that he – a pure Slovak! – covered the youngest Gypsy with kisses, on the cheek and on the mouth.

Our feet were itching. The Gypsies, regularly performing as street musicians in Vienna, offered the railway employee and me a juice-glass of champagne. »The last time you were a foreign element,« he told me before getting off in quiet Bruck an der Leitha. He was right. Like the Gypsies, I left the restaurant car at Petržalka. Now I know the local habits.

Since that time I have forced myself not to take that train. Wagon Slovakia on the Intercity 407 is a fixed ensemble. And we – we don't belong to the cast.

People's Body

That morning in autumn I am received by the friendliest village idyll I ever encountered in Central Europe. The sun breaks through the mist on the surrounding hills, a little stream whispers, two roosters walk about on recently cut wood.

Little houses with sharp gables made of dark wood from past centuries stand amongst functional houses of more recent origin. The amount of picturesqueness is just right. When I translate the name of the village, Hlboké nad Váhom, it sounds uncanny: »The Deep upon Váh«.

Hungry from the journey, I enter the little grocery shop Potraviny Mix to ask where one can get a breakfast around here. The 900-soul village is not equipped for tourists, I learn. No café, no restaurant, no B&B. The neat saleswoman spontaneously reaches for her private coffee tin and prepares a coffee for me, with milk and sugar. I buy rolls to go with it, she won't take money for the coffee. Additionally, she trains a young blonde from the neighbourhood, who radiates the fresh cordiality of a mountain pasture. They have a nice word for every customer.

I hike to the waterfall. At 10 a.m. sharp, an old hit song suddenly booms out of all the loudspeakers, loud and bombastic. One and a half minutes, then the Slovak love duet is abruptly interrupted and a woman's voice tells us the special offers of the day. Some older housewives have stepped into their front garden, standing in front of their flowerbeds with scrutinizing faces, and learn about washing powder and tomatoes. Again half a hit song, sudden interruption, a clicking noise, silence.

The natural spectacle of Hlboké is hidden in the forest. A smooth grey vertical rock face, the waterfall itself is overgrown with moss and doesn't gurgle too wildly. I refresh myself and walk back into the village, light and swift, back into the weekday-idyll, which I entered this morning with unease.

I am in the ethnically purest area of otherwise multinational Slovakia, in the national reserve of the Slovak nation. Here, the Slovaks are entirely themselves, among themselves, left on their own. And I have come here to understand the nature of bestiality. The bestiality that is represented by Ján O. and Ján S., the man-eater and the Hungarian-hater.

Ján O. is a young man from Hlboké, a handy carpenter who went to England for work. There, one day he assaulted the household of a retired couple and ate in the course of his attacks a finger, a cheek and a nipple of two old men. The victims survived, badly wounded. Ján O. is awaiting trial, charged with attempted murder.

Ján S. is the longtime head of the Slovak National Party, which has recently become a junior partner in the Slovak government. Incited by beer and cognac, S. badmouths Roma, gay people and women, but preferably the Hungarian minority, whose representatives he calls names like »lumpy«, »gauneri«, and worse.

The nationalists – also called »národniari«, »the folkish« – have their traditional stronghold in the Slovak national reserve. Recently, 12 per cent voted nationwide for the man who threatened to planate Budapest; in these districts along the upper Váh the percentage was 25 to 30. With two more villages, Hlboké holds the undisputed record: 38.82 percent.

Even though I only discovered Hlboké because of him, I don't ask about the cannibal. I don't go looking for his parents' house, which was shown in all the Slovak newspapers, and don't walk about asking the 26-year-olds what it feels like to have been to school with a cannibal. I don't want to know what makes the one that lost it tick. I want to know how the village thinks.

So I listen to the people: The migrating youth provide for their parents. The middle generation has work, but can barely live off it. The saleswoman, widowed at a young age, makes 180 euros, a worker at the highway construction site gets 230 euros. The mayor is a národniar and networks with the local národniari elites. They call his position »richtar«, and the learned plumber really gained glamour in 1998. It was then in a referendum that he accomplished the secession from BytĐa, the small town nearby that had previously incorporated Hlboké. The richtar supposedly financed his holiday house from local funds, people gossip. There are three things everybody gives him credit for: the water pipeline, the gas pipeline and the cable network.

I know I eventually have to ask them about the 38.82 percent. They may be as nice as they are, I can't spare them that. Revitalized by the waterfall, I feel strong enough. My mood is so excellent that not even a punch could spoil it.

I contemplate questioning techniques and choose the sledgehammer approach. In front of the Potraviny Mix stands a single wooden bench. Two rough, middle-aged guys sit on it, hands on their beers, clothes dirty. I approach them, look at them and wait until they interrupt their conversation. Without any further ado I come straight to the point: »Why do so many here vote for the SNS?«

The following pause seems long to me. »We are Slovaks,« says one of them finally, grumpily starring into his beer. He mumbles some incomprehensible things, which I take for curses, and ends the subject with, »Let's stop talking about politics!« Then he disappears.

The other one seems to like me, and before he goes behind the Potraviny Mix to pee, he politely asks me not to run away. Jožko has time, he works on the highway, he has no shift this week. I sit down and we talk, with a view of the city hall and the elliptically tarred bus turnaround in front of it.

It becomes evident that Jožko is everything I would not have expected in Hlboké. He despises the národniari and loves the Hungarians of Slovakia. In doing so, he divides mankind into two groups: Those he values he calls by their first names, those he criticizes he calls »prick«. He tells the mayor constantly: »Dušan, you are a prick«.

To get one over on the »whole gang«, Jožko votes for the Hungarian party, and when their chairman is on TV, he is on the edge of his seat: »Bela is a solid guy.« He pronounces the Hungarian first name with gentle familiarity, as if he and Bela had just plodded on the construction site for twelve hours.

Other villagers come by, like the wife of the only ethnic Hungarian who found his way into Hlboké. Her husband cannot work anymore, she complains, he might have his leg amputated. She complains about the welfare system and has already identified the culprit: Brussels. »The EU brought this upon us!« she exclaims – and, hence, proves European normality.

Meanwhile Jožko's revolutionary speeches become more enthusiastic, more malicious and more pricky with every Popper Beer he scrounges off me. I would have loved to stay longer, but a bus was ready to leave in front of the Potraviny Mix. And before any shadow could fall on that chaotic idyll of opposition, I preferred to be on my way.

Such a Glorious Place

Recently, the subject of a lecture lured me to Gänserndorf. I was heading towards a spectacularly sprawling district capital. Situated at commuting distance to Vienna, on the Eastern end of the urban continuation of Donaustadt-Deutsch-Wagram-Strasshof, the town attracts a lot of people.

In 1981, Gänserndorf had fewer than 5,000 inhabitants. But soon there will be 10,000. The new cooperative apartments are affordable and family-friendly, the flat landscape inspires one to go jogging and cycling. If the trend continues, we will soon all have to go to Gänserndorf.

I was a little late and asked for the way in the underground crossing of the demure train station. »There must be something special there today.« answered the saleslady. »You're already the third to ask today.« The answer electrified me. Apparently I wasn't the only one longing for the subject of the lecture, but with me the entire northeastern border region: »Cultural differences with the Czech Republic«.

Indeed, the hall was jammed with people. Almost exclusively men, well dressed, and in a superb mood. The lecturer was an engaging routinier with a healthy complexion and splendid white hair that could make one jealous. He had recently been to the »Tschechei«, to the Moravian Renaissance town of Telč, »such a glorious place, you can bargain magnificently with the people there.« He mainly sells agricultural machines to Ukraine.

The no-less-eloquent listeners bit by bit turned out to be salespeople, Austrian salesmen, roaming the East with their English. I learned that the market is »drained of top salesmen« and an American study had found that self-control was the most important success factor in selling.

I had walked into a lecture for salespeople. The cultural differences that might have shed light onto the twisted relationship between Austrians and Czechs shrank to a distribution-focused comparison between »Western Europe« and »CEE«. CEE includes over twenty nations.

I have learned that the »Easterner« has far more problems with self-esteem than his Western counterpart. »The Easterner lets us come. I speak and he observes me. He uses the time to observe me.« If he doesn't get a business card, the Easterner might get upset.

Despite all optimism, the following applies: »It will certainly take a couple of years until they have been parallelized.« Until that time, Austrians busily export the corruption they usually sneer at into CEE. »There is a directive in the finance ministry,« the lecturer said with a hushed voice. »If it is documented, a bribe can be set off against taxes.« He himself invites the Easterner to a seminar, in a good Austrian hotel. »Possibly he likes that even more than a money-goody or a TV set.«

I fled the genre picture at halftime and went to the Geyer. Following up on the trend, I know more and more people that have moved to Gänserndorf, and only had to wait for half an hour until one of my acquaintances had time for me.

Those who have not had to go to Gänserndorf yet might wonder why the café of a bakery chain turned into a widely accepted meeting point. Maybe it's the hearty service of the Slavic waitresses, maybe that's the Gänserndorf way of life. One day, we will all sit there.

In the Rose Garden

For years I have been drawn to this place, a little island in an enormous water storage lake. Often, I passed the lake and I saw, through a distant mist, the island where a little, lost church stands.

I was so mesmerized that in winter, I wrote at this place: come summer I would swim to the island. Shortly afterwards, a reader contacted me and offered his raft. By Whit Monday, my wish was fulfilled. We rowed towards the abandoned place. What I discovered was of such beauty, one should hardly write it in a newspaper.

The island is located in the South Moravian reservoir of Nové Mlýny. Three connected, cascading expanses of water stretch out for 32 square kilometres. I didn't know much more when we inflated the raft early that morning. The raft had some hundred valves and was a highly modern, splendid example of human navigation, designed by engineers of the US Navy.

I mainly knew that on Lake Nové Mlýny II any kind of watersports is forbidden. This is what the prohibition sign said that stuck out of the reed on the northern bank of the entirely overgrown lake, leaning lopsidedly forwards. »Nature reserve, no trespassing,« it said in Czech, »§ 34 of law N° 114/1992.«

Further, I knew that in the seventies, the damming of the junction of the rivers Dyje, Svratka and Jihlava had caused the flooding of a village. The parish Muschau had existed since 1276. Until 1945, it had been inhabited by 700 German-speaking South Moravians.

That Monday, a horrible wind was blowing. The waves on the southern shore seemed more peaceful, so we set out there only to end up swaying like a nutshell in the ocean. Shortly after our journey had started, my captain put on his flaming orange life jacket and yet another moment later he would have preferred to return. He rowed, I struggled to keep course with the helm and tried to avoid dead branches, breaking through the surface. To pay respect to the truth, we were not masters of the situation. We were driven towards the island.

The landing seemed plainly impossible. On a tiny neighbouring island, hundreds of seagulls were screaming over the thundering spray washing over the tree trunks. The island with the church was surrounded by reed. Further inland the vegetation was lush. I could not name it botanically, some sort of linden green giant weed, four to five metres high, blocking the view to the church. With effort, we paddled towards the shore that was protected from the wind. We pulled the raft into the reed and made our way through the tree-high weeds, a few metres uphill.

And all of a sudden it was bewitching. All of a sudden it was sunny and still, with not so much as a breeze. We stood among rich, blossoming rose bushes and the church lay directly before us. A church of

Romanic origin, with chipped-off plasterwork but intact structure. Gasping and thoroughly wet, we stumbled out of the storm and into the sweetness of a wild rose garden.

The tower was accessible. I had to duck when I entered the tower through a narrow iron spiral staircase, and then climbed up through a broader wooden staircase. I walked slowly and slightly anxiously. My captain had preferred to stay outside. The walls were covered with inscriptions, which calmed me down. It was all names and dates, most not too old, from the zero years.

When I reached the top underneath the intact roof, the wind was howling again, entering through the windows. A wooden shutter lay broken on the floor of the room, resembling the ribcage of a stranded skiff. The view was magnificent, the lakes, the seagulls, the Pálava hills with their vineyards.

I descended and entered the church. It had been totally emptied, a layer of crumbling plaster covering the floor. Just at the entrance there was a chiselled stone, the inscription in German. I could only decode the ending: »Saviour eternally. 1850«.

The walls were exposed to blank bricks at some parts, a few paintings could still be distinguished, maybe the patron saint of Muschau, Leonhard, also the patron saint of cattle. In the fresco on the ceiling, I could identify a kneeling angel.

To reach the choir, I had to fight my way through thorny undergrowth outside; the passage to the iron spiral staircase was completely overgrown. All walls of the choir were carved by visitors. Mostly Czech names:

»Marcela, Monika, Mira, Lenka, Radka«, but also »21.08.1991: Karsten, Jörg, Uwe, Jana«. Often, names of places were added, mainly of the Moravian surroundings, and dates: 15.07.1988, 30.07.1989, 18.03.1990. Almost all entries originated from the time before 1994, when Nové Mlýny II was shut down for the public.

The church was dry and it smelled nice. Even though the church is not a house of the Lord anymore, I did not have the feeling I was standing in a desecrated place. Among all the messages, I did not find any one of abusive or insinuating character. There was no garbage in the church whatsoever.

I lighted a candle in the place where the tabernacle once had stood and went out to the wild roses, to my captain who was sitting in the grass with a delighted expression on his face. We imagined how the village of Muschau might have looked. Only later, I would learn from contemporary witnesses that we were partially mistaken.

We thought the island of Muschau was the remains of the church hill. The communists saved it on purpose, however, constructing artificial banks, hence the vegetation we had to fight ourselves through. We did not know that the roof had been renewed after 1989 because the tiles had been stolen.

We did not know that the village had been levelled in the sixties, before it was flooded. The Czech settlers, who had to leave the village after barely 20 years, took apart the houses themselves. Most used the material to build a new Muschau close by in the village Pasohlávky, still bearing the name: Nový Mušov.

And when we were standing enraptured in the lull, I did not know Marie Landauf, a Muschovian born in 1916, who told me about her village. In 1960, fifteen years after her displacement to Austria, Landauf visited her now Czech village. The unknown Czech who lived in her parents house »thoroughly honoured« her, she told me. »He kneeled down before me and apologized with the words: I have to czechizise.« What became of him, she does not know. She never visited Nový Mušov. »It's an unpleasant feeling. One is at home and still feels like a stranger.«

We knew none of this when we animatedly hopped into the raft and left the island the same way we had arrived – drifting on the agitated lake. We landed happily on the northern shore, exactly at the prohibition sign, which we remembered as a good landing place. We pulled the plugs out of the hundred valves. Now we only had to walk the five kilometres to the car.

I got the hint from a well-informed friend. The leading positions in the intellectual scene in Slovakia, he told me, are held by Hussites. He enumerated a few names that rang a bell. My jaw dropped.

Hussites? Silent shivers went through me. How could contemporary Slovakia fall under such an influence, the ghost of the plundering, religiously and nationally outraged mob that infested my Lower Austria six hundred years ago with flails?

I went to the Sunday mass of these people. I found a modern church in a side street of Bratislava's old city. It was a generously expanded basement of an ordinary old building. The reception was located on the ground floor, the cloakroom was used by everybody. At the entrance stood a lean young man in a black suit and held out his hand to everyone: »Ciao, I am Josef!«

Josef was a »preacher« of the church that doesn't know priests. He had mailed me days before, saying that the connection between his Cirkev Bratská church and the Hussite movement had been broken in the 15th Century when their founding father, Brother RehoĐ, had refused to carry a sword. All fine and well, I thought. I want to see with my own eyes if those are really »Soft Hussites«.

Even though the charismatic star of the »brotherly church« preached in the countryside that Sunday, the church was full. Before me, a perfectly rehearsed programme unfolded, performed by neatly clothed laypersons of the upper middle class. They gained confidence by starting out with »Holy God, We Praise Thy Name«. Czech and English gospels followed, and readings in Slovak; English-speaking visitors were cared for with headphones from the interpreters' booth.

Someone said the Cirkov Bratska recognizes any kind of Christian baptism. The focus was on Josef's sermon, which he held in Czech. He spoke about the sacredness of the Sunday, well structured, thoroughly prepared, occasionally with mild humour.

The audience barely had to participate. There was no communion, which spared the community of Catholics, Protestants and seeking people at least one question. Most followed the service like a lecture. Some folded their hands, some crossed their legs, the girl in front of me rested her head on her dreadlocked boyfriend's shoulder.

It didn't get more Hussite. I attended a cultivated gathering of people among which many – a second car in sight – had found their second church. Not unpleasantly touched at all, I left the church, which has multiplied its followers to 10,000 in a few years. At the exit of the cloakroom the preacher shook my hand again: »Ciao, I am Josef.«

And then I found them, the true Hussites, the following Sunday. They were few, in a hidden chapel in the old city of Bratislava, congregants of the Církev Đeskoslovenska Husitská, who reveal in their name that they belong to Hus as much as to Czechoslovakia.

A striking number of men sat there in the rows of chairs. Severe, old gentlemen, sitting up straight, squeezed into grey suits, listening expressionless to the Czech-speaking priest. I stood in the door, the only young mother smilingly offered me the seat next to her children. But I savoured my Hussite-shudder, and before it started to wear off, I left.

The Third Attempt

Where the Danube makes a gentle bend, between dotted foothills of the Carpathians and the Slovak border, the beautiful town of Hainburg is situated. The city is 1,113 years old and is inhabited by a respectable minority of immigrated Turks. This raises the question of the Austroturkish-Slovak relations, but first I want to know something else from one of Hainburg's brightest Turks: How does he feel when he passes through the medieval Fishers' Gate?

Cengiz knows the inscription on the local memorial plaque there by heart, like a nursery rhyme he drones: »In commemoration of the residents of Hainburg, slaughtered by the Turks on the 12th of July of 1683 during the invasion of the town.«

That is exactly the problem, states Cengiz. He is young and eloquent, has learned Slovak, prefers Austrian newspapers over Turkish, and with his red stubbly beard, he could easily pass for an Irishman or a Lower Austrian. In the minds of many Hainburgers, the massacre of 1683 seems to have happened only two or three decades ago, he says. And on the other hand, many older Turks show little interest in their integration.

Cengiz meets me at the Turkish sports club, in a backyard in the old city. The trophies of a team that doesn't exist anymore are lined up above the counter. We drink tea from little, bulbous glasses. Turkish TV is on. Yellowing wallpaper shows a panorama of the Bosporus. Young and older men chat and play cards.

A woman only enters the sports club when Cengiz organizes a lecture, which is held by a woman. He volunteers in the community, and tries to promote literacy amongst mothers through a German course.

Once, he asked the local authorities for support. That was the moment when a little municipal council member pronounced a big quotation: »Ask not what your country can do for you, ask what you can do for your country!«

Hainburg has 5,600 inhabitants. According to the census 500 to 600 are of Turkish origin. All Hainburg Turks are from Eastern Anatolia. Some work in the

Hainburg tobacco factory, some in the filter plant, many at Vienna International Airport as baggage handlers or cleaners.

Since there is no nightlife in Hainburg, the young Turks used to go to Vienna a lot. Vienna is far, Vienna is expensive, so they started to go out in Bratislava. Slovakia has never been confronted with Turks. The bans from bars in Austria are not known there.

»Once we got a thrashing from Slovak skins,« Cengiz tells, who meanwhile has become the good husband of a Turkish wife. The blows, of course, where meant for another people: »Those guys called us dirty Italians.«

Apart from that, Austroturkish-Slovak relations are developing very promisingly. Half a dozen of Hainburg's Turks already speak Slovak. The limit is reached when a son introduces a Slovak girl to his father who wouldn't even want an Austrian one in the house. In the mind of the conservative Turkish father, Russian and Moldovan girls have crystallized as the women who dominate the brothels of the Turkish homeland. He will not be talked out of his belief that Slovak girls are whores.

Cengiz for his part is more focussed on Austrian-Turkish relations. The memorial plaque for the »residents of Hainburg, slaughtered by the Turks« – he has something in mind with it. Nothing that would put those Hainburgers off, who think they are experiencing the third Turkish siege. No provocation, a conciliatory gesture, a clever act. I know it already, but I can't tell.

Roma Road Show

Last Saturday I learned what sovereignty looks like – the sovereignty of a man. I went to the Roma Road Show in Kertváros, a scanty suburb of the tastefully ornamented jewel of a city called Esztergom. Everybody waited for Bódi Guszti, a beloved star of Hungarian Roma Pop music.

The long, even village meadow was secured with tape much like the area in front of the stage. About a dozen white Hungarian men in blue uniforms reading »security« supervised, with stern concentration, the driveway and stage, where enchantingly gifted Roma kids danced the opening act.

On this early Saturday evening, the eye of the stranger found everything it knows about the Roma people: a smoking grandmother, a pregnant teen.

At the stalls, chilled soft drinks and stringy schnitzel sandwiches, wrapped and sealed in plastic, were sold. Most drank cans of beer, but I could observe no excess whatsoever. Compared to a rural feast in Lower Austria, these some hundred Roma, who gathered in front of the stage, presented an example of well-mannered bourgeois behaviour. Few whites had found their way here: some drunken, tattooed, bleached, not exactly a selection of the Hungarian elite.

For quite some time there was no show, and then, Bódi came. He arrived in a convoy of black limousines, accompanied by his band and clan. From the black Mercedes with the black-shaded windows he himself emerged. »Bódi, Bódi!« the crowd behind the security fence shouted. Bódi waved two, three times, and stood around at the cars for another hour.

He was an unconspicuous character, wearing tight, black trousers and a T-shirt with a black and white pattern on a moderately stout body. For some time he disappeared behind a VIP screen, an octagon made of green fabric planted into the meadow. Most of the time, he had himself patted on the shoulder by a gentleman, who appeared to be the patron of the local Roma. This self-assured, middle-aged gentleman wore a white linen shirt hanging over his authoritative belly. Gold chains as thick as cables framed his neck and there were enormous sharp gold rings on his hands, capable of killing a bull.

Far away from it all, on an unpopulated stretch of the meadow, I saw a veritable Gypsy baron. He held court with his clan, on white historical garden chairs, immediately in front of the Dixi toilets. He wore a broadbrimmed, white straw hat. Once he got up and stretched his impressive belly towards the sky, yawning. At this moment, Bódi was already on stage. The Gypsy baron sat down again, thus demonstrating to his people that there was nothing he cared less for than this Bódi.

Well, Bódi's show was lame. He sang an anthem of a duet that features on his homepage, jumped about for two, three songs, intoned anew that same duet and went off.

The concert was free; no tapes or merchandise were sold. It was a display of plenty hiding its source. When the fans crowded around Bódi, who was already behind the steering wheel of his limousine, it became evident that the security had been hired to give way at the only delicate moment. Receiving the cheers through the open window, Bódi left the scene.

That was pretty much the moment, when the sovereignty of the gipsy baron suffered. Slowly he gathered his entourage, had the garden chairs moved onto the open deck of his truck and had boarded his Mercedes family van with poise. And still there was more dignity in this than a white man should think possible.

Martin Leidenfrost *was born in Lower Austria in 1972. He studied film and Slavic studies in Vienna and Babelsberg. He works as a screenwriter (Struggle, Cannes 2003) and freelance writer of essays, columns and feuilletons. Leidenfrost lives and works in Devínska Nová Ves, 35 km from Vienna. The World Behind Vienna – Fifty Expeditions, a collection of his literary commentaries, was published in 2008.*

Transitions Online, www.tol.cz, Czech Republic, 27 April 2007

Long-Distance Families (2007)

By Ana Maria Luca

Westbound labor migrants are leaving thousands of Romanian youngsters behind every year.

To reach Sperieteni, a village some 50 kilometers from Bucharest, leave the highway and drive half an hour along a dusty, unpaved road. Despite its remoteness, the village is infamous in Dambovita County.

»If you're looking for a place where only children and old people live, you have to go to Sperieteni,« says a woman in a village on the main road.

Indeed, the children here – as in many other settlements in the county – grow up virtually alone, many waiting for their house-cleaning mothers to call from Italy or Spain on Christmas, hoping to see them for perhaps two weeks during the summer holiday. Some wait to finish studying carpentry or another trade, then join their fathers on construction sites across Europe. Others end up in foster homes or even orphanages even though they have parents. And on occasion, a 10-year-old drops out of school, runs away from home, or even hangs himself in the closet with his father's tie.

The Romanian government estimates that 40,000 children have been left behind by migrants who go west in search of a job and money they cannot find at home. The actual figure may be higher. These are the children raised by mail, telephone, and even webcams.

But the parents' financial calculations wreak long-term havoc on their children: teachers describe assorted behavioral issues in the classroom, while of greater concern, hospitals in eastern Romania recently began reporting a rash of suicides and suicide attempts among troubled adolescents unable to cope with their feelings. While westward migration has been widespread over the past seventeen years, government officials and activists say they were unaware of any such crisis until the Romanian media first began highlighting the problem last year.

»We are devastated that 10- or 12-year-olds commit suicide because they cannot talk on the phone with their parents,« says local UNICEF representative Pierre Poupard.

Young and Old

Some child protection activists blame parents for limited understanding of their children's emotional needs and the stigma attached to any form of psychological therapy as a sign the person is »crazy.« And the problem of children left behind may soon grow

– if, as some observers predict, Romania's accession to the European Union this past January encourages countless more Romanians to emigrate.

For a Frenchman like Poupard who came to Romania to monitor children's rights, the tens of thousands left in the care of relatives – and deprived of that special parental bond – are quite unique. »It's an alarming phenomenon,« he says. »But we cannot judge anybody. We need to understand first. In Romanian society, there is the idea that a child's upbringing needs only material things: a roof, food, and schooling. But the parents have to understand that a child needs his or her mother.«

Sperieteni itself hums on a springtime Saturday afternoon. The road is full of boys playing soccer and girls skipping rope. Old women sit on small chairs in front of their gates, sighing from time to time, keeping an eye on their grandchildren. They don't talk to strangers readily. The words come heavily.

»Eh, most of the young ones have left, more than half the village,« whispers an old woman in her seventies, sitting alone under a blossoming cherry tree. »A few have taken their children with them. But the rest live with their grannies. It's so difficult to live here now. I am old and at my age, it's not easy to take care of the house and these girls.«

Indeed, her daughter, Liliana, left her two daughters, 12 and 9, with her two years ago when she went to Spain to work as a housekeeper. »She had to,« her mother laments, her voice rising as she paints a picture of parental sacrifice. »Her husband left her. We had no sign of him for years. She had nothing to do here, in this village. She had to go to get money and raise these girls properly.«

Soon the old woman returns to her own troubles. The girls »are so difficult to raise,« she says. »Liliana sends money every month, but it's still difficult. I am ill ... I don't know what to do with them. I would give them to an orphanage, but they won't accept them.« A state institution would only accept the girls if they were orphans.

By now all the children in the neighborhood have surrounded the old woman. Her granddaughters have taken their place by her side. As their grandmother calmly admits to having considered giving them away, the girls look down.

»I miss Mom,« says Nicoleta, the older sister. »Most of the children in my class are home alone – 15 out of 20. I hope my mom will come home to take us with her. I saw her once this year on the webcam. It didn't work very well, but we saw each other. I want to go live with her. She promised to come home at Easter, because she couldn't be here on Christmas.« She seems calm, perhaps trying not to cry in front of strangers. »I want to go and work there with Mom,« she says. »But I have to wait and finish high school first.«

Sperieteni mayor Marin Voinescu's papers document just 100 people who have left the village of some 2,000 for Spain. »I'm glad they left,« Voinescu says. »They have saved me some money from the budget. They all relied on the social programs.« Local women typically work as maids in Spain, the men on construction sites. However, the mayor asserts, »We don't have abandoned children here.« With scientific precision, he states, »Out of 100 people who left, four have taken their children with them. We have three children at the orphanage in good conditions, and the rest are with their grandparents – who are young and healthy, physically and psychologically as well.«

Voinescu notes that children whose parents work abroad are better dressed at school and often envied by their classmates. Anamaria Neagu, the village English teacher, agrees. Yet their classmates' envy only adds to the children's sorrow, Neagu says: »Most of the children at school have both of their parents away. Grandparents and aunts take care of them, but this is not enough for a child. The teenagers often have behavior problems – they are violent, they skip school.«

She talked to some parents about their children's problems, but they weren't receptive.

»They don't seem to believe the kids are acting this way because they don't have parents at home,« she says. »They are not all very educated people. They worked all their lives. They grew up alone, too: ›Remember when our parents used to work double shifts in the factories during Ceausescu's time, and we would play outside with the apartment key hanging around our necks? If we survived, why can't these kids manage it?‹ That's what the parents say. Most of them chose to work abroad, to live in the outskirts of Paris or Rome, to save money and support their children. And they expect the children to understand this.«

Getting Rid of the Jobless

Sperieteni and Dambovita County are hardly unique.

In other parts of Romania, like the impoverished Moldavia region, Italy is more popular, especially for nurses and women who care for the elderly. Numbers are difficult to assess. According to an Open Society Foundation study, more than 2.5 million Romanians – one in nine – currently work abroad. Many took their children with them and moved away for good. But most only go for a couple of years and leave the children behind, believing they are safer at home, in school, in the care of relatives.

The national Authority for the Protection of Children's Rights estimates there are 13,000 families with either one or both parents away, leaving some 40,000 children in a relative's care. But Authority spokeswoman Cristina Niculescu asserts the numbers are far from the reality. The statistics, she says, rely on the good will of local officials to count these children. And many did not answer the government's demand to send accurate numbers.

On 26 April, the children's authority raised its estimate to 60,000 children whose parents currently work abroad.

Her boss at the Authority, Bogdan Panait, expresses his frustration.

»Most mayors believe ... they are getting rid of the unemployed and won't have to spend the budget on stipends for the poor,« Panait says. »And there is the mentality that there is nothing wrong with the grandparents raising the children.« But he says the generational gap should not be underestimated.

Observers suggest the government is at a loss over the situation. But Panait says the children's rights authority is trying to cope, issuing an order in June 2006 for child-protection agencies nationwide to count the children left alone and monitor them. Yet, there is no deadline and no sanction against agencies not doing their job properly.

The children who cannot be cared for by relatives should by law be placed in institutions or foster care. But, according to the Authority, only 600 children of 40,000 are now in this situation. These are the truly abandoned children. Their parents left for good, typically disappearing without a trace, so the state stepped in. The others are only to be monitored by the few and poorly paid social workers.

»Moreover, the government recently prepared a new draft law on preventing child neglect,« Panait says. The bill would set up some ten specialized offices and information centers to help the children whose parents left to work abroad. But it's a long way from becoming law.

Another tool to keep track of children left behind is the requirement that migrant workers who find a job through government agencies must give the name of the person caring for their children. Some 40 percent find a job through such agencies. The children of the rest, those who inform no official bodies they are leaving, are most in danger, Panait says. »We are trying to find a solution for the problem, but it is rather new to us,« he says. »This phenomenon has been going on for years now. But we became aware of it just a few months ago.«

The Search for Alternatives

Child care professionals and the general public both became aware of the phenomenon early in 2006, when the media revealed several suicides among such children. One 11-year-old boy who had lived for two years with a foster family in a village in Iasi County was found hanging from a beam in the basement. It shocked the public. He was well taken care of, the media reported, but missed his mother. This March, a 16-year-old girl in Campulung Moldovenesc, in northern Romania, hanged herself in the bathroom, reportedly because she had low grades and didn't want to disappoint her father, who was working in Italy.

It took the exposure of these deaths for child protection workers to link migration with adolescent suicide. The problem appears to be larger than anybody thought. According to a study released by the Social Alternatives Foundation in Iasi, a quarter of the children left by parents skip classes or drop out of school. Moreover, some 30 percent of juvenile delinquents have parents working abroad.

Over the past year, the situation in eastern Romania has been even more dramatic. Dozens of villages are populated only by children and old people. In Iasi County, a local hospital has estimated that every four days, a schoolboy or girl tries to commit suicide. The psychologists at St. Mary Children's Hospital in Iasi have so far treated eighty-nine children for life-threatening overdoses of pills. Many tell doctors they miss their absent mothers and fathers.

A hospital spokeswoman says the staff is struggling with the epidemic.

»We have the psychologists, and these children get therapy here, but it's not enough,« Dr. Catalina Ionescu says. »They should be in therapy after they leave the hospital, too. And they can't, because they come from rural areas and most people [there] think that if you talk to a psychologist, you must be crazy.«

Meanwhile, just a handful of nongovernmental organizations and concerned individuals are searching for a solution of their own. To date, the Social Alternatives Foundation is the only NGO to request UNICEF's help.

UNICEF's Poupard says he hasn't seen anything comparable among other emigrants: »I'm sure that if you ask a mother from any other European country, ›Do you want to leave for the United States, for Japan or China, and leave your child behind?‹ I'm sure she'll answer, ›Are you crazy? I would never leave my child for all the gold in the world‹ ... People from North Africa migrate in great numbers to Western Europe. But the pattern is different. First the man goes, works for a couple of years and then he brings his family over. But the mother always stays with the child.« In Romania, though, women leave first, because it's easier for them to land a job as maids or caretakers of the elderly. Poupard insists that Romanians need to change their mentality. »A child needs the mother, needs love; it's only natural,« he says. »Putting a child in an institution is not the answer. We need to assess the cause, understand, and then do something. Explain to parents what their kids need. Talk to the children. Contact the parents and tell them the kid is in trouble. There are ways.«

Neagu, the English teacher in Sperieteni, says she would never leave her little boy, Mihaita. Her husband left for Spain in May 2006. Their 13-month-old, she says, has only seen his father once since, on the computer, and cries »Daddy, Daddy!« every time the phone rings. Yet Neagu says she knows dozens of children less fortunate than her child. At least Mihaita has her to hold him when he cries.

Meanwhile, she's saddened to see some schoolchildren around her falling apart.

»They have money,« she says, »but what's the use without a parent's love?«

Ana Maria Luca *was born 1979 in Romania. She studied journalism and mass communication at the University of Bucharest and at the Center for Independent Journalism in Bucharest. Today she works as an international news editor for Romantica TV. In 2004 she was awarded with the Young Journalist of the Year special prize by the Freedom House Foundation.*

Slovenské pohl'ady, Slovakia, May 2006

Central Europe – Lost, Found and Lost Again? (2006)

By Gustáv Murín
Translation by Bea Baloghová and Diane Seo

It is hard to determine when the term »Central Europe« first appeared, and who invented it. This idea challenged the balance of power after World War Two and struck a chord with Central European intellectuals who felt betrayed by the political separation of West and East in Europe. The term started to be widely recognized after revolutionary events in former communist European countries. In 1989, simply dividing Europe into the West and East no longer made sense. In the summer of 1998, the Austrian Cultural Institute in London organized the Festival of Central European Culture. Organizers invited artists from Austria, Croatia, Slovenia, the Czech Republic, Slovakia, Poland, Hungary and Italy. But this is precisely where we face serious difficulties with the term »Central Europe«. The question is whether these are the only countries that fit this term or whether others should be added? And if so, which ones?

In 1997, the respected U.S. travel publishing house, Lonely Planet, published a book entitled *Central Europe on a Shoestring* covering the following countries: Germany, Liechtenstein, Switzerland, Austria, Hungary, Poland, Slovenia, Slovakia and the Czech Republic. The term seemed to perfectly fit the »traditional German concept of ›Mitteleuropa‹, reliant on economic and geopolitical dominance« as described by Emil Brix in a special issue of the publication *Occasions* entitled Central Europe, published for above-mentioned cultural event in London (The Austrian Cultural Institute, London, 1998). Between the two World Wars, there had even been a tendency to characterize Germany as a holder of »Kultur« (culture) which ran counter to the Western tendency towards »Zivilisation« (civilization). But according to Milan Kundera (The New York Review of Books, 7/1984), Central Europe is »boxed in by the Germans on one side and the Russians on the other«, where »the nations of Central Europe have used up their strength in the struggle to survive and to preserve their languages. Since they have never been entirely integrated into the consciousness of Europe, they have remained the least known and the most fragile part of the West – hidden even further, by the curtain of their strange and scarcely accessible languages....«

Kundera's description automatically excluded Germany from the scope of countries covered by the term »Central Europe« (not to mention his confusing remark about it as »the most fragile part of the West« – in fact, he understands Central Europe as »the eastern border of the West«). But according to a precise reading of the above statement, Central Europe also excluded all German-speaking countries. This point of view would reduce the number of countries from the nine featured by Lonely Planet to five. Another American publishing house, Welden Owen, published a book of pictures edited by Jan Morris entitled *Over Europe*. In the chapter »The Central Europeans«, only Czechoslovakia, Poland and Hungary are listed. Of course, this 1992 publication did not reflect the split of Czechoslovakia, but if the author had been aware of it, he probably would have known that the Czechs don't like to include themselves among »Central Europeans«. They desperately want to be recognized as an integral part of Western Europe to the extent that in the last few years, their government has sabotaged most of the activities of the so-called »Visegrad Four«, the group of countries accidentally also covered by the publication *Over Europe*. So, from the purest point of view, does Central Europe only mean three countries – Poland, Slovakia and Hungary?

In his essay, »The Central European Dream« (in E. Busek and G. Wilfinger (Eds.) *Aufbruch nach Mitteleuropa: Rekonstruktion eines versunkenen Kontinents*, Vienna, 1986), György Konrád estimates the population of Central Europe to be between 100 and 200 million people. It is a very rough estimate, but certainly more than Poland, Slovakia and Hungary put together. So where do all of these Central Europeans live? In a publication mentioned above, Emil Brix tried to specify that Central Europeans live in »parts of Europe extending from Poland to Bosnia and Herzegovina and from Austria to the Ukraine«. Thus, we now have two more candidates for the Central European club who were missing at the presentation of »Central European Culture« in London – Bosnia-Herzegovina and the Ukraine. Brix was well aware of the eccentric position of the Ukraine when he wrote that »academics in the Western Ukraine are putting stress on Central Europe traditions, because this helps to overcome the lack of European contacts acting from a Soviet past.« And he suggested even more when he defended the position of Austria within Central Europe. »Because of the cultural traditions, Austria is a Central European country. The same holds true for the northern parts of Italy where the challenge and magic of borders is ever present,« he wrote.

The Vilenica Festival is a respectable annual literary gathering for Central European authors. Its Slovenian organizers included Italy as a matter of course. Furthermore, they included Germany in their scope, added all three Baltic States, and are currently pondering the question of whether Romania is a Central European country. Ultimately, the area we are dealing with ranges from just three to up to no less than sixteen countries covered by one geopolitical and cultural term. Consequently it could include 55 million people or far more than 200 million estimated by György Konrád. However, Milan Kundera was very well aware of the flexibility of the practical realization of »The Central European Dream« when he wrote: »Its borders are imaginary and must be drawn and redrawn with each new historical situation.«

At least one solid point?

Aristotle once said: »Give me a solid point and I will move the Earth.« Isn't this the solution to our problem? The newly discovered term »Central Europe«, frequently used in the media, calls not only for the immediate definition of its borders but of its center as well. So, frankly speaking, where is the center of Central Europe, or better yet, where in fact is the center of the Europe?

To answer these questions we first have to deal with the vague term »heart of Europe«.

During the years of existence of the former Czechoslovakia, Prague was constantly called the heart of Europe.

Surprisingly (or not), a poster at the international airport in Budapest in 1996 welcoming me to Hungary described the whole country as the heart of Europe.

However, according to the official bulletin of Adria Airways, Slovenia's national airline, Slovenia's Adriatic coast has aspirations to bear this proud title too.

Air France, on the other hand, offers flights connecting you to any place in the world from the heart of Europe, which, of course, is France.

The same thing is said in Luxembourg and the Netherlands.

I also heard a BBC political commentary about some political turbulence in Italy, to which we must pay attention because Italy is in the »heart of Europe«.

But The Times in London published a story about Bosnia with the headline »European heart in American hands«. And Americans took it seriously because President Bill Clinton referred to Bosnia as the heart of Europe too.

Last year while visiting Warsaw, I found a book by Norman Davies with the title *Heart of Europe: A Short History of Poland* in a book store called Megastore.

In the book *Storm of Globalization* (Jamex, 2002), Professor Ivan A. Đarota seeks to oppose self-deception of »geopolitical disorientation« when Belarus is presented as center/heart of Europe.

With a heart in so many places at the same time, it is not surprising that Europe is so close to a heart attack at any moment. But this is not the end of the troubles relating to the issue of the center of Central Europe. Of course, as befits such an important issue, we also have the officially claimed »centers of Europe«. There are three. Plus one.

With the help of the government, a hall was built in Krahule, in the central part of Slovakia, commemorating that village's central position in the continent.

However, in the Ukraine, the eastern neighbor of Slovakia, in the city of Rahov (south-west of the more well-known city Lviv) a pillar of stones was built showing the place where the »center of Europe« certainly is.

It seems that the Ukraine's neighbor, Lithuania, never heard about this, because people there have their own stone pillar. This one was erected in 1991 and was precisely located by the French National Geographic Institute at 25"19' latitude and 54" 54' longitude.

These three »centers of Europe« create a triangle with sides not shorter than 375 km – 750 km – 875 km.

However there is still one more. In the small village of Tállya in the Hungarian part of the Tokaj wine region, you will be greeted by selection of its special wines. And at the end of your visit, you will automatically receive a »certificate« claiming that you have visited the »Geodesical Center of Europe«. There is no explanation as to how they came to have this proud title. But certainly they believe in it.

Does Central Europe exist at all?

In the hope of finding a positive answer, but giving up hope of finding its precise borders and center, we come back to Kundera's definition of Central Europe and repeated by Emil Brix broadly as a »cultural landscape between Germany and Russia«. Rudolf Chmel, a Slovakian scholar, diplomat and Minister of Culture, tried to impose an element of time to this definition when he once said: »Central Europe is like an accordion. When the Germans and the Russians are doing well, they come closer and Central Europe starts to vanish. But when they are in trouble and withdraw to their inner borders, Central Europe suddenly emerges«. Today, Germany still has trouble with the reunification of the western and eastern parts of the country, and Russia seems to have trouble with everything. But, one day in the future when they have resolved their problems, should we expect Central Europe, regardless of the flexibility of this term, to vanish again? When will the future of Central Europe be finally liberated from its fatalistic past?

Gustáv Murín *was born in 1959 in Bratislava, Slovakia. Author of more than 1000 articles in Slovak and Czech newspapers, magazines and the international press. Author and moderator of TV series and radio programs. Interviews with Czech, Polish, Slovenian, and Slovak writers, journalists, theatrical directors, actor, non-fiction writer, playwright and scientist. More than 80 interviews with scientists from Slovakia, USA and Japan. Member of the Slovak Syndicate of Journalists since 1995. President of Slovak P.E.N. Centre (2000 – 2004), the worldwide writers' organization for freedom of expression.*

ORF, Weltjournal, Austria, 2005

Moldova – Left Behind (2005)

By Katinka Nowotny

0:07

It is six in the morning in Zirnestri, a small village in the South of Moldova, close to the Romanian border.

0:12 SOUND

0:17

Just as he does every other day, Anton cooks the breakfast for his younger brothers and sisters. Since his mother left five years ago to work in Turkey, he has been the head of the family.

0:32

The four children have had to raise themselves. Their father is an alcoholic and is rarely at home. And the last time they saw their mother was two years ago.

0:50

Anton Niculita, 16 years

ANTON »I remember how beautiful my mother was. I miss her so much. All the children who have a mother don't know how lucky they are.«

Nicoleta Niculita, 9 years

Nicoleta: »I last saw my mummy on the 20th of December five years ago. My younger brother and I were crying, but our older brothers made fun of us.«

1:10

»She packed her things and went across the field. That was the last time I saw her. She just went away.«

1:25 SOUND

1:27

Anton and his siblings are not an isolated case. According to Moldova's ministry of education, 30,000 children have been left without parents, who have left – often illegally – to seek work abroad. These so-called »social orphans« live with relatives, in orphanages and sometimes even alone.

1:42

They are emigration's forgotten victims.

1:47

The children have to take care of the animals on their little farm before they head off to school. They named their calf »Marius«. No one needs to tell them what their daily chores are. They know them well enough already.

2:05

Andre Niculita, 13 years

Andre: »No, we don't cut school. Sometimes I have to get wood. Then I can't go. But otherwise I always go to school.«

2:14 SOUND

2:21

Everyone in the village knows these hard-working children. They are role models for other children who grow up without parents.

2:32

Their daily journey to school isn't far.

2:35

Here, too, the poverty is palpable. The school has no heating.

2:42

The toilets are shabby outhouses.

2:45

And there's certainly no such thing as a school gym kit.

2:53

In Anton's class, the children are learning about the recent EU expansion.

3:02

On being asked how many children have parents working abroad, almost one third of the class gets up.

3:14

3 children in school:

Boy: Sandu Crafil

»My mother left two years ago to work in Turkey.«

Girl: Alina Caranfil

»My mother left three years ago and is taking care of elderly people.«

Girl: Natalia Ezanu

»My mother worked as a waitress in Romania.«

3:23

The same is true in Anton's brother Costa's class. For these children, left behind in poverty-stricken Moldova, childhood is all too fleeting.

3:33

Maria Girnet, 15 years

»My father has been working in Greece on a construction site for the past 3 years. He calls regularly, but I miss him very much.«

3:45 SOUND

3:50

Nadejda Dobanda, Teacher

»On the outside Anton looks like an average child,

but inside he is already a grown-up. He has so much responsibility. He has to take care of his younger brothers and sisters, and sometimes he does not have enough time to do his homework. In the past 5 years he's become very serious and solemn.«

4:09 SOUND

4:12

Moldova was once a prosperous country which supplied the Soviet Union with many of its goods. But these glory days are long gone: the economy is in a state of shambles, the factories are closed, and there are no jobs. To the east there is a volatile conflict over the secessionist region of Transnistria, which has frightened off Western investors. The only way out is to flee abroad.

4:34

Heidi Burkhart, Hilfswerk, Austria

»About 20–25 percent of the population have left the country, especially from the rural areas. That means that the fields are lying fallow, and the children stay behind. A quarter of the population! You can imagine what economic effect that has on a country.«

5:00

This is already the poorest country in Europe, and here in Southern Moldova, the poverty is extreme.

In the small town of Zirnesti, half of the inhabitants live beneath the official poverty line of a dollar a day.

5:15

Where parents are missing, grandparents often have to step in to fill the gap. Five of Anica's seven children work abroad. At 86, she hadn't planned on being a mother again. But she has no choice. Now she prays she'll stay healthy long enough to keep on looking after her grandchildren.

5:32

Anica Miron, Grandmother
»The mother of these children, my daughter, is a doctor. But despite the good education she still had to go and work abroad. The government does nothing to help us. Even if you are highly qualified, that doesn't mean that you will find a job that enables you to feed your children. I see no future for my children.«

5:54

There are just old people and kids in Zirnestri now. And the few people of working age left are scrabbling for their chance to leave the misery and squalor behind.

6:07

Taisa Lucinschi, Accountant

»You need 2,500 dollars to cross the borders illegally and work in Europe. If I had the money I'd be gone already. In this village alone, half the population has already left.«

6:23

The abandoned children have to make the best out of their situation.

6:32

Their chores are evenly divided.
They clean the house, cook and wash their clothes.
Their biggest pride is a well that they built themselves.

Anton Niculita, 16 years

»I built this well with my brothers. (PAUSE)
We dug for one week. It's 7 metres deep. We also made these rings ourselves. But we need concrete for 10 more rings, then we'll be finished.«

7:15

Their income comes from the little money they earn from their greenhouses. Here they plant tomatoes and peppers. Everyone lends a helping hand. The revenues are small.

7:28

Depending on the harvest, they earn between 150

and 350 dollars per year. The money has to pay their bills: the food for the animals, clothes for themselves, and supplies for the school.
But they have each other, their friends and the community.

7:43

Other children are less fortunate. They end up in an orphanage, like this one run by UNICEF. Our visit had been announced and the kids were all dressed up for the occasion.

7:54

There we meet Kolya. His mother became a victim of human trafficking.

8:02

Kolya Nicolae, 10 years
»My mother froze to death because she wanted to cross the border, to work illegally in Italy. She gave her bag to the smuggler, so that he could take it across the river. But he never came back. My mother froze to death in her clothes.«

8:22

The children on our farm have got used to their hard life.

MUSIC

8:39

Andre

»I wish Mother would come back. She said she would come for Easter, then for Christmas, but she never came.«

8:50

Life is tough for these kids, but they are modest and hardworking. Even the gift of a soccer ball is like manna from heaven. Imagine if they got their parents back.

END: 9:07

AKM: CD 02-30033
Music by Michael Lorenc film music »Bastard« 1997 Boje Buck Production
Coloseum Schallplatten GmbH
2) Elena's dance
5) Elena's theme on Dulcimer
21) In Elena's tunnel
23) Elena's dance

Osservatorio Balcani online magazine, Italy, 18 April 2008

L'amico americano (2008)

By Azra Nuhefendic

The cornerstone of the new American Embassy in Sarajevo has been laid. The building is to be erected on the city's most beautiful and central spot. Right next to President Tito's monument.

I'm sure that if Tito were alive, he would approve of his new neighbors. He made peace with the Americans in the early 1950s, following the split from the Soviet Union in 1948. Tito refused to subjugate Yugoslavia to the power of the Komintern, an international organization that unified the communist parties.

Tito's *nyet* to Moscow caused an earthquake in the Communist bloc, applause in the West, and a tempest in Yugoslavia. The Yugoslavian communists, educated to admire and accept without question everything that came out of the Soviet Union, suddenly found themselves in a serious dilemma: mother Russia or Yugoslavia.

Those not quick enough to switch over to the prevailing view ended up at Goli Otok – a Yugoslavian Gulag.

Why my father did not end up on that island remains a family mystery. He was a relentless Russophile. Furthermore, it seems that it was impossible for him to love one side without hating the other. He couldn't stand anything that came from the capitalist world, above all from America. Everything, including the English language, was mere propaganda, and as such, to be avoided at all cost.

In the 1960s the first American programs appeared on television in Sarajevo. My father spoke foreign languages himself – French and German - but we weren't allowed to watch English programs on television. Upon hearing even a few words he would shout: »Turn it off!«

Bonanza was very popular at the time. This was a kind of cowboy soap opera, which for us was a real discovery after the films about the invincible partisans that we were used to seeing. I still remember this show, but only for the trouble it got me into.

I was complaining because my father would not let me watch it. I turned my back on him and cried bitterly. He was aghast that something coming out of America could inspire such rebellion, and before I knew it, he slapped me twice.

His ideological convictions cost us a lot of money. At school, needless to say, I studied Russian. But soon we realized that one would not go very far in any career without any knowledge of English. At first my parents quietly paid for private lessons out of their own pocket and later I paid for them myself. This went on without my father ever officially acknowledging it.

Over the years, his aversion to English and the Western world in general subsided, but Russia, and all that goes with it, never lost first place for him; or not quite.

During the last war in Bosnia, my father remained in Grbavica, a neighborhood in Sarajevo that was occupied by the Serbian nationalist and paramilitary forces. My father, and all of his Second World War partisan comrades, be they Serbs, Croats or Bosnians, were offended, betrayed and humiliated by the behavior of the nationalists, who, as the saying goes, »raised their guns against their own brothers«.

Shortly before Sarajevo was reunited, Russian soldiers arrived in Grbavica as part of the United Nations Protection Force. My father expected them to come as benevolent liberators who would finally correct errors and restore order.

But the comrades, *the batjuška*, arrived holding three fingers in the air, the sign made by the Serbian paramilitary and almost any other criminal who had come with the intent to steal, molest or kill. The Russian soldiers openly expressed their affinity with the Serbs.

Apart from the beginning of the war, the most dramatic period for the people who remained in Grbavica was during these two months before the reunification of Sarajevo. The Serbian paramilitary forces rushed to steal or destroy everything they had not stolen or destroyed during the previous four years.

Everyone was in danger in Grbavica, including the Serbs who refused to leave. The Serbian propaganda encouraged them to leave, and to destroy everything beforehand so that it would not fall in the hands of the *balije*, a derogatory term used to describe the Bosnian Muslims. Some of those who decided to leave Grbavica even opened the tombs of their families to take away the remains.

During this period the neighborhood of Grbavica resembled a tragic biblical scene: widespread panic, last-minute crimes committed in haste, trucks and animal-drawn carts full of stolen goods, people mourning their long-buried dead. It was like the Bosnian saying: »Good times for bad people.«

During one of these evil nights of total darkness, not only because of the lack of electricity, but for what was happening to the people, the Serbian paramilitary forces parked a truck in front of a half-empty building. They entered my father's apartment, locked him in the bathroom, and passed the whole night calmly carrying away what remained: heaters, lamps, pictures, windows, pots and pans, beds, couches, rugs, linens, and personal objects such as the medals that my parents received for their bravery in the Second World War. The electronic and kitchen appliances had already been stolen at the beginning of the war.

Every so often the criminals would enter the bathroom. My father would rise and they would order him to sit down: »If you stand up, old man, I can't cut your throat«. They searched for money that he did not have.

Before they left at dawn, they set fire to the apartment with my father locked in the bathroom. He was saved by friends and neighbors. A Serbian family kept him hidden in their own home for a month. They all risked getting killed if they were caught.

All of this we learned much later. We spent five days without knowing what had happened to my father. Five days of anguish, of panic, frantically trying to understand what we must do and how to do it. All we knew was that he had disappeared.

I recalled that an American colleague named Dan, a fellow journalist, was in Sarajevo, but on the other side, which was controlled by the central government. With great difficulty I managed to contact him using a satellite telephone, a very rare and expensive device in those days. Another American named Laura was involved in this desperate search. I begged them to do something for my father.

Dan risked his life in the chaos that reigned during those days in Grbavica, and went to look for my father in an armored vehicle supplied by the High

Commission for Refugees. The first time he did not succeed. He found the apartment empty and in ruins. The second time he managed to discover where he was hiding and found him alive. Dan gave my father 500 dollars - a fortune that in those circumstances could potentially save his life.

This is the story that came to my mind while I was reading the news that the Americans were building an Embassy in Sarajevo.

Today I hope, as do most Sarajevans, that the Americans will finish the building as soon as possible. One of those typical high-rise facilities, a kind of fortification, with five floors underground and ten more above, complete with bunkers, secret passageways, and the latest spy technology, even weapons – whatever they want. Because with this news comes the precious message that the Americans intend to stay in Bosnia. As the ambassador, Charles L. English, confirms: »We believe in the future of Bosnia and Herzegovina as an independent, stable and multi-ethnic state capable of taking its rightful place in European and Euro-Atlantic structures.«

As for my father, I do not think he would object. He survived the war, he saw Sarajevo reunited, and lived to see the family come together again after five years of being spread out over three continents and five countries.

And, as for me, I witnessed my father sharing a *slivovica* (plum brandy) with his American friend Danny. My father slapped him on the back, saying something that in English would be »friend, friend«. And than he let me translate their conversation. He spoke in Bosnian and then patiently listened to the English version, nodding his head in agreement.

***Azra Nuhefendic** has lived in Italy since 1995 as a refugee. Contributing writer: Osservatorio Balcani web magazine. SUD European Magazine. Il Piccolo, Trieste; Journalist: Radio & TV Belgrade (1992-1982); Sarajevo's daily Oslobodjenje (1982-1977). Awards: Premio Dario D'Angelo, the best non- Italian journalist (2004). Special award for covering of the uprising in Romania (1989). Annual Radio & TV Belgrade Award (awarded twice, 1986 and 1987).*

Monthly economic journal »Piaţa Financiară«, Romania, January 2007

Romanians Accessorized with Bulgari(ans) (2007)

By Octavian-Dragomir Jora

Clamour. Champagne. Fireworks. Happy New Year(s)! Twice. Perfect opportunities for us to get drunk, both »democratically« and »liberally«, as if to quench the thirst for Europe of each of the two parties forming the liberal-democrat »oil and water« coalition. As liberal-democracy is the edge of modern times, a phenomenon from which we have been trying to sober up for seventeen years, eyes swollen. We raise the blue flags – garnished with the compass rose or with the yellow stars – instead of putting basil on Christian icons and we congratulate one another when the bitter sweet »euro spank« sounds noisier as it hits the »wide neckline of the Bulgarians« than when it slaps the »small Romanian foreheads«. We have completed accession!

University Square / Revolution Square for us (as we have a bipolar coalition) and Battenberg Square for the Bulgarians were shaken by the »hurray« of some crowds for which entering the EU looks astonishingly similar to what was once »the escape to the West«. Two Eastern nations, neither in a hurry nor too misfortunate, have defected together all the way to the civilized universe of the Union.

Thirty million »Joe Bloggs«

Boring raw data: the accession of these two nations to the big European household may look like two poor, starving relatives at the family Sunday barbecue. Figures talk about the 30 million souls meant to enrich the Union – or rather ruin Europe as it is seen from the camp of »social bohemian euro-citizens« who despise the alleged fund-cravers, labour market-disturbers and job-crushers. Too few are those who see the newcomers as net added value.

With 22 million inhabitants, Romania becomes the seventh most populated country in the EU, which means half the Polish demographic contribution and twice the Czech or Hungarian peoples. With 46 per cent of its population living in the countryside and sharing 4 million »petite« agricultural estates and with 22 per cent of its inhabitants subsisting below the poverty line, Romania scares Europe. As do the 2 million supposed »expats« gone to pick berries in ... Iberia.

By Union standards, Romanians and Bulgarians are poor and disrupt the harmony of the EU's economic indicators. Per capita GDP is just a little over one third the EU average. Wages are Lilliputian, with monthly averages of 250 euros in Romania and 180 euros in Bulgaria. However, compared with the EU's snail pace, the newest pieces of Union territory are moving quite rapidly: 7 per cent economic growth in Romania and 5.5 per cent in Bulgaria in 2006.

Heartaches can be seen before handshakes as the big accession arrives. Heartaches: the Bulgarians need to shut down six reactors at the Kozlodui nuclear power plant and they are also obliged to modernize fifty-five aircraft to bring them up to EU standards. We too, we have to work hard to improve our customs oversight as we became one of the external frontiers of the Union. Moreover, we need to deal with some phytosanitary »small change«, and we are also expected to implement a minimal anticorruption regimen.

The East comes with a dark side

Romania and Bulgaria's member state résumés are »glorious«. Commercially, the two countries only account for 0.8 per cent of exports and 0.7 per cent of imports in the EU-25 trade balance. One possible strong point: the unit labour costs in Romania are 80 per cent of the EU-10 average, and those in Bulgaria come in even lower at 46 per cent of Eastern Europe's labour market standard.

However, relocating the industries of »Old Europe« is a process that depends on many different factors, including the improvement of the entrepreneurial framework, stimulated by convergence with communitarian habits. For now, doing business in Romania and Bulgaria is at least encouraging, though not brilliant, says the World Bank.

Yes, European money will spread in the two economies. In the EU enlargement's accounts, they are posted as a current cost burden that will be redeemed in the »long-long run«. Which means that there is no really enthusiastic news for the net contributors to the EU coffers. These two countries are craving cohesion funds »thanks to« the current development disparities. However, this alleged panacea is capped at 4 per cent of the recipient's GDP, which means an average of 4 billion euros for both Romania and Bulgaria.

Romania is waiting for 17.6 billion euros in structural funds and 12 billion euros for the development of its agricultural sector during the 2007–2013 financial period. Bulgarians can only hope for less because of the smaller size of their economy. Direct payments for agricultural activities will rise gradually over the next decade until they reach EU-15 levels, while structural funds will decline between 2007 and 2009 to prevent »transfer addiction«.

How to Get Rid Of the EU Smirk

Romania has been allocated 3 billion euros and Bulgaria 1.5 billion euros in the first three years. They also have to contribute over 1 per cent of their GDP to the common budget, which means 800 milllion euros for Romania and around 200 million euros for Bulgaria. Older members are concerned about over-funding the New Europe, while the Easterners fear they will be able to absorb too little of this bargain. And it was considered to be a good reason to introduce protection measures to head off the risk of becoming a net contributor.

As usual, the »stakeholders« are many and anxious where public money is concerned. The EU's reforms might be affected by the less-developed newcomers, so Westerners look on Romania and Bulgaria with a critical eye. Both countries have enough reasons to support the extensive common agricultural policy and its measures for regional development, bolstering the ranks of those opposing plans for substantial reforms.

And there is always »economic nomadism«, which could be translated as the liberty of circulation for the labour force, unless this refers to the Easterners »sick« with social dumping, which is a major European fear. The EU Commission estimated in 2004 that the EU-10 will send between 70,000 and 150,000 migrants to the EU-15. Today, rumour has it that over 600,000 »expats« have gone to the UK alone over the past three years.

A fear of immigrants from the small oriental »barbarian« side of Europe led some Western governments to make their labour market filters harsher. The most hysterical in this, the ex-liberal British, are also seen as euroskeptics and balkanophobes in the media. On the other hand, Sweden and Finland keep their doors wide open, which might be a sign that their welfare states need some fresh meat. Both Bucharest and Sofia say that the migration tsunami may have ended by now.

EU Money, and »Down the Tube« Potential

As succulent as the financial package that is meant to support the EU-2 may seem, there are fears about the money not ending up where the original projections intended. This could happen either because of institutional inability to manage the funds, or because of inclinations towards »informal practices« amongst the »ex-communist business elite«, as Tom Gallagher, an expert on Romanian transition, called our entrepreneurs.

Practically, Romanians could receive 1.7 billion euros in their first post-accession year. Bulgarians stand to receive much less, just 661 million euros. But the EU's confidence in Romania's capacity to honestly and efficiently manage those funds is good for 84th place (of 164 economies) in the Transparency International Index. That is behind China and Cuba.

Being the most corrupt country in the EU, Romania has a matching partner in the Balkans. In Bulgaria, gangs made up of members of the former Soviet services control a large part of the economy. And local authorities haven't been able to convict even one of the 150 suspects involved in Mafia-style crime since 2001.

Western governments live in fear that once accession has been obtained, along with EU money, reforms will slow down. Brussels is, therefore, determined to punish such misconduct by preparing to apply safeguard clauses that could make the newcomers less comfortable with their new status as a member state of a Union less and less welcoming of new guests that come and stay for lunch.

Ricardo Economics, or the Reasons Why We Simply Cannot Starve in the Single Market

Among the economic criteria for EU accession, the one concerning the necessity »to cope with competitive pressure and market forces within the Union« is often understood as if there were some sort of »natural inability« to deal with this competition that will doom us unless the omniscient and omnipotent authorities take the appropriate measures.

In order to erase this heresy against common sense, we can resort to a heavily unexploited and improperly grasped economic theory. Taught to exhaustion at the economics universities, Ricardo's theory of comparative advantage remained broadly misunderstood and its lesson rather unassimilated (especially by those who see the market as a device that can't live and breathe without politicians' consent).

This »classical« theory – by no means obsolete because of this but refined up to present days – teaches us that a country is competitive in relation to a foreign partner even if it is less productive technologically – that is it produces everything at higher costs than its rivals. Okay, but »honestly«, one may ask, »what does Ricardo have to do with Romania or Bulgaria?«

»First and foremost, this theory shows us that although in the highly improbable event that a country has no absolute advantage in any sector of the economy (simply put, everything it produces is more expensive compared to other competing countries), it is practically impossible to not have at least one comparative advantage, that is to be »less disastrous« in at least some industries. The market sceptic who thinks that Romania or Bulgaria are in such a lousy position must be prepared to demonstrate and argue that the rest of the EU is exactly »n« times more productive than Romania or Bulgaria at any good imaginable! It would be a one in a zillion chance! (If we speak with a minister, he must have been taught this vulgarly simple economic reasoning; if not, he had better keep his mouth shut.) Romania and Bulgaria do have industries that, when let run free, could develop externally by themselves, and this to the benefit of all involved, both the EU-25 and the newest comers, argues Mihai-Vladimir Topan, a young researcher at The Ludwig von Mises Institute in Romania.

The second greatest thrill is the following: Where exactly does Romania possess comparative advantages? This question is not the smartest one. »The comparative advantages are attributes of Romanian individuals or companies, not of a holistic entity called Romania. And much more importantly, if we can demonstrate that there are necessarily industries that have comparative advantages, we cannot put a finger on them *ex cathedra* or ›ex ministry‹. Only from the activity of private undertakings can these successful industries arise. There is no other way out,« concludes Mihai-Vladimir Topan.

If some could be irritated by the idea of the harsher competition that Romanians are expected to face in the single market because it is believed that »we could reach the position of not being able to produce anything, becoming ›their‹ débouché«, they commit a serious flaw. Romanians could definitely produce competitively in certain sectors, and this will profit us all– the other Europeans will in their turn have the opportunity to produce the goods in which they are most skilful. Of course, some Romanians could be irritated by the idea of shifting back to the activities where the comparative advantages are sustainable on their own. If they ask not to be removed from their field of activity at the expense of European consumers and taxpayers, then it is their demands that should be considered inappropriate and harmful.

»The EU itself does not spare us from demagogy. On one hand, it strictly regulates sectors such as agriculture, imposes environmental standards sometimes exceeding economic logic and thus limiting free competition, and on the other hand, it serves us the ›cope with competitive pressure and market forces within the Union‹ menu. We may tell them to relax: We will be able to cope with that; it's the nature of the free market. And definitely let the unfettered business environment freely select its industrial champions,« Mihai-Vladimir Topan agrees.

Octavian-Dragomir Jora*, born in 1980 in Romania, assistant at the Faculty of International Business and Economics in Bucharest, chief of the foreign affairs department of the monthly economic magazine Piaţa Financiară. Great Award of the Young Journalist of the Year contest (Freedom House and Edipresse AS Romania) in 2007, first prize at the Reporter European Contest (European Commission Delegation in Romania) in 2005 and second prize in the same contest in 2006. Various articles in economics publications.*

IWM Post, www.iwm.at, Austria, 2005

The Horrors from the East (2005)

By Wojciech Orlinski

Visiting a bank in Vienna, I noticed a multi-lingual message with lots of flags of the Central and Eastern European states. Among them, there was a flag of my own country, which was a nice welcoming surprise. It was accompanied by a message in Polish saying, »The safety vault is automatic and alarmed. Our employees cannot open it.« It was a rather clear message about what sort of guests from our region this bank is expecting.

As early as the 18th century, the West imagined Eastern Europe as inhabited by savage people, wild beasts, and supernatural monsters. There is for example Count Dracula, located in Transylvania by the imagination of the Irish writer Bram Stoker in 1897. But the horrors from the East are also prominent in popular culture created locally. Victor Bocan, the Czech designer of the video game Operation Flashpoint, portraying the Russian invasion of a small fictitious country (called Republic of Nogova and strongly resembling the Czech Republic), said in one interview: »Obviously, Operation Flashpoint: Resistance is a realistic game; so forget zombies, ghouls or giants, although I have to admit that some Russian officers are really evil.«

Metropolis Software, the Polish developers of another computer game set in Poland – Gorky 17 – went a bit further in terms of the Eastern horror. The storyline is set in 2009, shortly after the admission of Poland to NATO and the EU (it is quite ironic that when the game was being designed in the late 1990s, both seemed to be matters of the distant future; the game was actually released the same year Poland joined the NATO). A special task force of NATO troops is sent to investigate a secret Russian military facility near the Polish city of Lublin, known under the codename Gorky 17, only to discover that Russian experiments on genetics and mind control have bred monsters of various kinds. Gorky 17 was successful enough on the international market to justify the release of two sequels. From my point of view, it is interesting that Polish and Czech game designers aiming for the global market consciously (and maybe to some extent cynically) take advantage of the stereotypes of the East to win international recognition.

One of the wittiest examples of the »fear of the East« is the fake tourist guide *Molvania: A Land Untouched by Modern Dentistry*, written by a trio of Australian TV comedy producers. The guide looks very much like a real tourist guide, with maps, photographs, and suggestions of where to eat or stay. However, the fictitious Central European state of Molvania turns out to be a real house of horrors. Most of the jokes included in this book revolve around the same scheme: having described something that actually might be a genuine tourist attraction, the authors finally turn it into a grisly joke. For example, when describing the beauty of the Vzinghta Gorge, the authors mention a »spectacular cable car« that »sadly no longer operates,« but you can still admire a »memorial plaque dedicated to the service's last 23 passengers.«

The authors' immense imagination saves this scheme from becoming monotonous after a few repetitions. But the story always remains the same: in a nice restaurant, guests are reminded to tip their waiters generously as they carry concealed weapons. An interesting ski trail leads through a minefield. The country capital is worth seeing via bicycle – and an English language brochure on this subject is readily available at the casualty ward of the local hospital.

Partially, this usage of the »Eastern horror« comes from the fact that this book is actually a two-layered joke. It is not just a parody of Central and Eastern Europe, but also a parody of a certain style of tourist guide, in which the hardships of travel are presented as an attraction in themselves. Nevertheless, it is very interesting that the authors of *Molvania* have chosen Central and Eastern Europe, in particular, as a background for this parody on how to make your travel unnecessarily tough and dangerous. Tom Glaser, one of the trio of authors, explains it this way: »We trace the origins of ›Molvania‹ to a trip that the three of us made over a decade ago to Portugal. It might just have been a coincidence but every monument or tourist attraction we visited seemed to be closed for repairs. At one point, we started making up fake guidebook descriptions. (...) When we eventually got around to writing the book, we decided to place our fictional country in Eastern Europe because we figured no one was too sure of the exact geographical boundaries in that part of the world.«

It turns out that the real inspiration for Molvania was actually Portugal – a country located as far to the west of Europe as is geographically possible. In fact, experienced travelers can see that many of the book's photographs were actually taken in southern Italy or on the Iberian Peninsula. But the Australian authors are right to talk about geographical ambiguity »in that part of the world«. One can safely assume that no other part is so densely inhabited by countries that are solely a figment of the imagination.

Apart from the fictitious states already mentioned in this paper, there are also Slaka, invented by British writer Malcolm Bradbury; Orsinia, created by the American science fiction writer Ursula K. Le Guin; and Vulgaria, where the British writers Ian Fleming and Roald Dahl located some parts of their book for children, *Chitty Chitty Bang Bang*. Video game designers also seem to enjoy locating their fictitious states on this part of the globe – apart from the games that we have mentioned already, there is for example »Republic: The Revolution«, designed by Elixir, a game that simulates leading the democratic opposition in the »Post-Soviet Republic of Novistrana«; and Volgia as the setting of a dark political thriller videogame, »In Cold Blood« by Revolution Software.

Comic book fans will certainly know the Central European states of Syldavia and Borduria as the settings of popular volumes from the Tintin series by the Belgian author Hergé. And one should not forget Krakozhia, home of Victor Navarski, the main protagonist of a recent movie by Steven Spielberg, »The Terminal.«

And last but not least the kingdom of Ruritania, first mentioned by Anthony Hope in his novel *The Prisoner of Zenda*, but then used by various authors whenever they needed an imaginary country for their narrative (including economists from the Austrian School).

These imaginary states are usually created by people of the West; frequently, while they are ostensibly located somewhere to the East, they are actually used by the West to depict the West in disguise – just as Molvania is really Portugal. The same happens with countries that do exist in reality. One of the best examples is Bram Stoker's Transylvania. Needless to say, Stoker had never been to Transylvania, nor had he any particular interest in that region. As we know today, he originally considered the Austrian province of Styria to be the birthplace of his famous bloodthirsty count, whose name was supposed to be simply »Count Wampyr«. However, he accidentally found a mention of »Voivod Dracula«, with the explanation that Dracula means »devil« in the local language of the Wallachians – thus Count Wampyr changed his name and moved with his coffin about a thousand kilometers to the East.

While Vlad Dracula was indeed a historical medieval ruler, he has no visible connection with Bram Stoker's Dracula, just as Bram Stoker's Transylvania has little to do with the real region, now a part of modern Romania. In Stoker's novel, the young solicitor Jonathan Harker travels east to Transylvania hoping to strike a good deal on real estate with the mysterious Count. As a result, he finds himself imprisoned and haunted by female vampires. He bravely manages to escape their charms, but Count Dracula arrives in England. Lots of horror and carnage on English soil follow, but it all ends well when Jonathan, acting under the firm guidance of good old professor Van Helsing, manages to chase Dracula back into his castle and finally kill him for good.

Sexual innuendo throughout the book makes it obvious that the story is not about Eastern Europe, but about the subconscious fears and desires of Victorian society. Thus, the stereotypical portrayal of the Eastern horror is not about Eastern Europe, it is about the West looking for skeletons in its own closet. This is even more obvious in the case of the book's unofficial movie adaptation, »Nosferatu,« shot by F.W. Murnau in 1922. As was aptly demonstrated by Siegfried Kracauer in his book *From Caligari To Hitler*, German expressionist horror movies were portraying the fears of the German middle-class in the Weimar Republic, fears that culminated in putting blind trust in Hitler as a sort of alleged Van Helsing who promised to chase the dreadful eastern monsters back to their homelands. It is even striking to what extent the visual language used to create horror in Murnau's »Nosferatu« resembles the language of Nazi propaganda.

Stoker's Dracula and Murnau's Nosferatu« present the stereotype of the Eastern horror in its purest form. It can be described as: 1. A young and naive Westerner invites someone from the East or accepts an invitation and travel eastwards (or both); 2. Something terrible happens because of this mistake and he suffers greatly; 3. Other Westerners also suffer or their lives are in jeopardy; 4. Luckily, under the guidance of an experienced and wise representative of the Western civilization, the young and naive Westerner is able to repair all the damage he has caused.

During the Cold War, this scheme was often repeated in James Bond spy thrillers, where agent 007 was playing the role of the experienced and wise representative of the Western civilization, whereas democratic Western governments were cast for the »young and naive« role, as they foolishly allowed refugees from the East – such as Max Zorin or Auric Goldfinger – to settle in the West and run their profitable businesses, while it's all too obvious that these businesses are nothing but a cover for their real activity in Soviet intelligence. Finally, some kind of Van Helsing must arrive and save the day – Western civilization prevails in the end.

This scheme makes it easy to understand why the authors of the guide to »Molvania« chose this particular region. If you want to make a macabre joke about a young and naive Western tourist who went somewhere to see great vistas and subsequently died in a cable-car accident, it's natural – and stereotypical – to make him travel to Eastern Europe. In reality it could also happen in – say – Italy, but it wouldn't be as funny, as there would be no appeal to the stereotypes we all have in mind.

By saying »we«, I mean also those who live in Central and Eastern Europe. We get the joke and we laugh at it, because – to quote Mayakovsky – we think it's »not about us, it's about our neighbors.« Poles will think that Molvania is actually Belarus, Czechs will locate it perhaps in Slovakia, and Hungarians most probably will say it's very much like Romania. We all know the »fear of the East« as it is something deeply rooted in our own popular culture. And in fact, it is something significantly older than popular culture itself; its origins can be traced to the ancient times and the period of the barbaric invasions from the East.

This stereotype unfortunately has visible political implications for the contemporary European Union. After all, the idea of enlarging the boundaries of the Union is all too similar to the first part of the »eastern horror« stereotype, when the naive Westerner invites someone from the East. Economists and politicians say that it was a rational thing to do – but the subconscious fear of those raised on spy thrillers and vampire tales also takes its toll.

To quote The London Times from March 24, 2005: »France heaved a sigh of relief yesterday after it emerged from the European Union summit in Brussels that President Chirac had won his battle against the monster that has been terrorizing his country. The creature's name is Bolkestein's directive (...) Frits Bolkestein, a Dutch member of the last Commission, merely sought to implement a 45-year-old commitment to open European frontiers for the service industries that now account for 70 per cent of its economy (...) Left-wing opponents have succeeded in demonizing the directive as the harbinger of the hell of ›social dumping‹. In the popular view, this means invasion by cut-price Polish plumbers, Estonian electricians and Slovenian surgeons, who will push French professionals out of business.«

Anyone who has ever tried to find a good plumber in Warsaw must at least giggle trying to imagine something like a horde of Polish plumbers invading France, especially when you consider that all of them would have to speak French fluently enough to apply for a job in this language, while in fact finding one that would speak proper Polish might be difficult enough. The fear of francophone Polish plumbers is no more rational than fearing Nosferatu or James Bond villains. However, it is not just the French who are haunted by these nightmares after 2004 – nightmares of monsters likely to come from the East. Since in reality we cannot hope to be saved by Professor Van Helsing or Commander Bond, the least we can do is to inform these monsters in their native language that the safety vault is automatic and alarmed.

Domino weekly paper, Slovakia, 1 August 2002

The Seventh Lack of Power

(WINNER 2004)

By Luboš Palata

Sabina Slonková: »The thought that somebody could want to kill me simply because I wrote a few lines about him in the paper seemed quite simply absurd.«

We have achieved nothing. For members of the Mafia we are nothing, and today the communists laugh about us. The privatisation enthusiasts, who acquired the majority of that which belonged to everybody and which should have been distributed to everybody, are set up to the end of their lives, the lives of their children as well as their children's children.

And the politicians? They view us as tiresome pests that have to be chased away if we become too importunate. For some premiers we are the greatest idiots in the country.

Our readers, listeners and viewers read, listen and watch us and then they go and vote in complete contradiction of what we have been advising and recommending all these years.

Our best years, when we still had the offers for fabulous positions at our feet, are long gone. The fishpond in which respectable journalism is still conducted to some extent is drained again and again. Some do not survive and commit professional suicide with a leap to the opposite bank and the air becomes scarcer and scarcer for virtually all those that remain.

We are getting older, having families, putting on weight and also becoming a bit comfortable. Routine has replaced imagination, life is characterised by tiredness rather than enthusiasm.

We wanted to make sculptures or at least vases, but the most we manage under the conditions granted to us is cups. Craft becomes mass production bearing the label »hand painted«.

We do not even manage to budge the world that we wished to change, and on top of everything we now know this. People demand that we be police officers, judges, foreign ministers, brokers, art connoisseurs and trainers but we are not one iota better than the clerks in a bank.

We have an idea of how things should look here but we have no idea where we could get the people who are capable of implementing these ideas. We no longer have any illusions about those who were at the rudder, are there or would like to be there – we have known them far too long for that. Our belief and our enthusiasm have been disappointed and we have disappointed with our belief and our enthusiasm.

We have made mistakes so often that we can no longer even remember how often it was. We also got things right sometimes, but nobody can remember that either.

We know how goods should be procured, to sell the people who own newspapers, radio stations, television. We know that our customers cannot be satisfied because we buy ourselves from time to time and know that often one can neither read oneself, listen to oneself nor watch oneself.

The Seventh Lack of Power

We should be the seventh power and at the same time we know that on two hundred and ninety nine days out of three hundred we are only the seventh lack of power. If crooks did not let other crooks get busted so that it looks as though they were smaller crooks, although in reality they are bigger crooks, we would not have this one day out of three hundred.

The more our ideas, our energy and our enthusiasm flag, the more we smoke and drink and the more tranquillisers and sleeping tablets we take. We have ten or twelve years behind us in which we were able to do proper journalism. If the statistics do not lie, then we have a maximum of twenty years left before we come to a miserable end.

Until the last moment when we are carried out feet first, we do not give up hope of being worth at least enough that someone who is actually an even bigger bastard longs to kill us for that which we have succeeded in doing to him.

Luboš Palata. *Born in 1967. Writer, journalist. Studied political science and Central and Eastern Studies in Prague. 1990–1993 foreign affairs editor for the daily newspapers Občanský deník and Telegraf, as well as at the Czech TV station Česká televize. 1993–2001, editor and commentator for MF Dnes; 2001–2003, Central European correspondent for Hospodáiské noviny; 2003–2005, Deputy Editor for the Slovakian daily newspaper Pravda. Currently editor of the Czech daily Lidové noviny.*

Prager Zeitung, Czech Republic, 28 February 2002

The View from my Window in Bratislava (2004)

By Luboš Palata

The borders become hazy in the distance: a panorama of the triangle of land situated between Austria, Hungary and Slovakia.

Bratislava, Pressburg, Poszony – three names, three cities and yet one and the same. In clear weather I can see three countries from my apartment in Bratislava. Austria is on the right – the imposing Roman garrison town of Carnuntum, the metropolis of the province of Pannonia Superior, was located there within sight 1,700 years ago. Today, not only the massive ruins of the triumphal arch, which are at their most beautiful on a sunny morning against the yellow rape fields, but also the Roman road, the amphitheatre and the numerous sculptures, graves and other excavated items that can be seen in the museum serve to remind us of it. A vast Celtic oppidum was located on the hill opposite, which rises from the banks of the Danube above the picturesque, medieval little town of Hainburg, long before the Roman period. Celts also settled directly in front of my window. When the house in which I live was built, the grave of a Celtic warrior and a small amount of golden treasure was found here. But it was not a big town. The main oppidum on my side of the river was situated 20 kilometres further north on the Danube at its confluence with the Morava. This place, however strange it may seem, forms the border between Austria and Slovakia today. This is also a consequence of the defeat of Přemysl Ottakar II in the battle on the Moravian plain 800 years ago. That defeat laid the foundation for the emergence of the great Habsburg dynasty, a line that ruled half the world. Today, the Habsburgs are still represented by two members in the European Parliament, one from Germany and one from Austria.

Bratislava's Venice

From my window I can see Austria as far as the castle above Hainburg and, if the weather is nice, as far as the Burgenland mountains, which run from north to south along the Austro-Hungarian border. It is not just fantastic wine that grows in the mountains but also picturesque Austrian villages, interspersed with Croatian and Hungarian ones. From my window, Hungary looks like an endless flat plain, which gives a presentiment of the mountains surrounding the capital Budapest somewhere in the distance. Below me, at night, I can see the lights of the Slovakian residential area Petržalka, which is alleged to be the largest new housing estate in central Europe.

The »concrete Bronx«, as the housing estate is also known, has made what was the small city of Bratislava after the Second World War into a metropolis with 500,000 inhabitants. At the end of the 1960s, when the construction of a residential area was considered, there was also a project that envisioned the construction of a small, Central European Venice. Artificial canals from the Danube were supposed to stretch between several storey, modernist blocks. Then the Soviet tanks arrived and asphyxiated not just the »Prague Spring« but also »Bratislava's Venice«. Instead, the Communists and their initial successors following the Velvet Revolution of 1989 created an artificial lake known as Gabčíkovo. It lies surrounded by alluvial forests on the eastern edge of my field of vision from the window and from here, on Napoleon's Hill, it looks as though the sea begins here and not 1,000 kilometres away at Constanca in Rumania. According to old inhabitants of Pressburg, only east Slovaks – that is, people from Košice, Prešov and even further away, who, as people say here, »have not got as far as Bohemia« – live below in the new housing estate of Petržalka, where the freedom won twelve years ago is only visible in the level of the rentals and in a few supermarkets. They are viewed somewhat contemptuously by the descendants of the bourgeois city of Bratislava that was destroyed and where 80 years ago 80 per cent of the inhabitants were Germans and Hungarians and only 20 per cent were Slovaks.

The Hungarian remains Slovakian

This city had already been gradually disappearing when it was given the name Bratislava after the founding of Czechoslovakia in 1918, but it went definitively with the end of the Second World War, which also rounded off the old world after an intermezzo of 20 years. The Germans disappeared and before them the Jews and after these two groups the Hungarians went as well. But today a trace of the multi-ethnic life of the first half of the 20th century still beats in the picturesque, little capital surrounded by new buildings and by motorways. In Csemadok's dance hall, in the cultural association of Hungarians in Bratislava, forms are currently being completed for identity cards for Hungarians living abroad. »We do it differently from the Slovaks,« reports a grey-haired man. »To obtainrecognition as a Slovak living abroad, they had to be able to prove their Slovak descent going back three generations.« To become a Hungarian it is enough to speak a few words of Hungarian. You do not need anything more. Eighty years ago, virtually everyone fulfilled this condition in the city, which was the place where Hungarian kings were crowned for over 300 years. Today people only occasionally come to Csemadok's premises. And the majority who could be Hungarians do not even apply for the identity card. They could travel through Hungary almost free of charge with the identity card, they could visit museums, galleries and theatres free of charge. Perhaps they are simply too lazy or they do not want to lose 30 minutes filling in forms. They already get enough forms from the Slovakian government. Or there is another reason: with its project to unite all Hungarians in the Carpathian basin, the Budapest cabinet of Viktor Orban, even though it only has 30-year-olds in it, simply slept through the time: the time when it was still important whether the town with the glorious view was called Bratislava, Poszony or Pressburg, when it was still important which borders lead where in Europe and when it was important for people whether they were born as Slovaks, Hungarians, Germans or Czechs.

Daily »Lidové noviny«, Czech Republic, 21 June 2004

Hundred Year Old Tower Blocks and Austrian Student Fraternities (2004)

Central European notes by Luboš Palata

I imagine that Vladimír Špidla was the person at the entire EU summit in Brussels most cursed, not just by our editorial team but also by the editorial teams of other European papers. The »ringleader of the orphans«, as we re-baptised him here that Friday evening, did not achieve anything either. Since if Schröder and Chirac once thump the table with their fists and announce that they will not withdraw one step further, then not a step will be withdrawn. I originally wanted to travel to Prague but because the summit ended late I made my way to Vienna after a little while, which is after all somewhat closer to Bratislava.

The primary reason for spending a summer Saturday in Vienna was the exhibitions. I do not know how these Austrians do it but on that day alone I was able to gaze at Rubens, Warhol, Schiele and Kandinski, to name only the most famous artists. I parked in an underground garage below the museum quarter, behind the back of the memorial to Empress Maria Theresa. In front of the museum, however, I immediately took my shoes off to be able to walk on a twenty-metre-wide map of the world, which rounded off an exhibition of enormous photos in the style of the »National Geographic« that was also installed on the pavement.

The view from Kamchatka over Europe was thrilling and yet again confirmed for me the fact that the name given to this little piece of earth (on which we had disputed the constitution on Friday) in China or Russia is correct. They simply call it the »European Peninsula«.

After a little searching, during which I passed under the windows of Pavel Kohout's Viennese apartment, I came upon Kandinski. The walk through his exhibition was not merely good for the soul; it also reminded me how open Europe was at the end of the nineteenth and beginning of the twentieth centuries. Wassily Kandinski (1866 – 1944), the Russian painter, was able to stay in Germany or Switzerland without any restriction and then return to Russia where – Bolsheviks coming and going – he could continue painting. Having spent half of my life to date under Hussák's communism, this still seems miraculous. For my son's generation this will perhaps become a matter of course again. Of all the pictures – and there were a few dozen of them in the exhibition – Moscow's Red Square, dating from the period immediately after 1900, captivated me most. Apart from the domes of orthodox churches it also showed – unbelievable though this may seem – tower blocks.

Eventually it was six o'clock, and so instead of having a look at the Rubens (as originally planned) I continued my journey to Bratislava. The route towards the airport went past the most interesting house in Vienna, an experiment by the painter and architect Hundertwasser. It offers not just a pretty exhibition of his pictures and architectural designs but also a pleasant café decorated in green. After a coffee, which was most welcome given the impressive cultural experiences I had undergone, came my punishment in the form of a one-hour traffic jam on the motorway leading to Budapest and Bratislava. There, where a gigantic Roman triumphal arch from the third century of our calendar stands beside the open road to Hainburg, I turned off to the little town of Bruck an der Leitha. I have travelled along this road for years but this is the first time I have turned off.

I did not regret it: medieval town walls, an imposing church, a whole row of beautiful, old and even slightly dilapidated houses, a palace that can scarcely deny that it once was a castle. And also a wonderful advertisement on which the firm Zamecnik (»castles« in German) announces that it does carpentry.

It was cosy – even a little kitschy – sitting in the castle restaurant among all these arms, swords and shields. However, the greatest experience awaited me in the lavatory, through whose walls I could hear German nationalist protest songs through the neighbouring salon. A beer festival was taking place here, organized by a »student fraternity« , one of the nationally focussed student associations that emerged a hundred years ago here in Austria and whose original aim was to conquer the Slavic peoples and unite all Germans. Today they still wear historical uniforms with sashes in the German national colours. What their goal currently consists of is the question here.

I made my way through the silently sleeping Austrian town to my car and contemplated the mishmash in my head: Špidla, student fraternities, Hundertwasser, Kandinski. Europe. A snapshot of the centre.

Transitions Online, www.tol.cz, Czech Republic, 31 January 2008

Serbia: Not Quite Online (2008)

by Larisa Rankovic

Within Europe, Serbia lags behind regarding the use of technology to streamline its government services. But change is coming.

The small city of Indjija is a magnet for foreigners. Last June thousands of people literally invaded the city when the American band Red Hot Chili Peppers gave a concert, and in recent years businesses have been tempted to invest in its industrial zones with tax holidays, and promises of an »efficient and business-friendly environment.«

The town, with a population of 53,000, is located 40 kilometers north of Belgrade, has developed a reputation for its cutting-edge technology – especially in a country that still mainly uses paper and bureaucratic queues are a common sight. Indjija's government directories and services can be accessed on its official website. Here the 33-year-old mayor of the city, Goran Jesic, points out that the town's »System 48« e-government service allows businesses and residents to process permits and get help through the Internet – within 48 hours. Mile Bodrozic, chief of the Department for Information Systems and Communications, said the system model was originally developed in Baltimore, Maryland. The American city officials used it to disseminate information from the city's police and later expanded its application to other departments. The World Bank says that e-government – the delivery of information, records, and services to citizens and businesses through the Internet – improves transparency and efficiency, while at the same time reducing the likelihood of graft. Filing taxes, obtaining permits, paying fines, and receiving answers on questions such as where to recycle old household appliances, are just a few examples of what e-government can do.

Indjija is not the only city in Serbia in which efforts are made to harness technology in order to make government tasks more efficient and easily accessible. The western city of Valjevo lists contact information for more than 350 local administrators, data on available building plots in the area, and local laws and regulations. Valjevo was among the first to provide online voting information, although it is still not possible to cast a ballot electronically. That could change in due time. At an e-government conference, Milan Markovic, the Minister of Public Administration and Local Self-Government, said he hoped that Serbians living abroad would be able to use Internet voting in future elections. There are approximately 37,000 registered voters who live abroad. Not all of Serbia is as advanced as some of its municipalities, and many citizens still spend a considerable amount of time filling out paper documents and going to real, rather than virtual, offices.

In a survey conducted in 2005 by the UN, Serbia ranked 40th among 42 European countries regarding e-government preparations. And among the 179 UN member states providing services online, Serbia ranked 156th. The UN technology report consequently advised Serbia to increase investments to to provide citizen services on the Internet. However, even if more e-government services were offered, only a few people would able to access the Internet. In 2006, only 13 percent of all Serbians had access to the Web, a percentage well below the European average of 43 percent. Aleksandra Smiljanic, Serbia's Minister of Telecommunications and Information Society, acknowledged the challenges of expanding services through the Internet at a technology conference in Belgrade last October. She said more resources would be invested to improve online services and thereby reduce paperwork and storage – and to bring the country in line with European Union standards. Last year, Serbia joined the EU's Competitiveness and Innovation Program, which requests further investment in technology and the provision of public services on the Internet. Furthermore, it must approve laws on privacy and data protection.

Not ready for E-Government

Even the Serbian Ministry of Telecommunications and Information Society is lagging behind. In its first three months of existence, the ministry, which was created last year, had no website, and even today some government ministries still do not provide e-mail addresses. Whcn asked for the reaons, Nebojsa Vasiljevic, Deputy Minister for Telecommunications and Information Society, said: »I believe that people in these ministries do use e-mails, they just did not publish them on the website. Maybe that was done on purpose.«

Vasiljevic added that there may be some misunderstandings about the e-mail services, as some addresses were not published with the »at« symbol. This was a common practice used to deter e-mail spam. »I have received many comments that the e-mail addresses on the ministry's website included ›at‹ instead of ›@‹. This was done on purpose, to make it more complicated for programs which collect e-mails through websites and then send spam. And it is even safer not to publish on websites at all.«

While some local authorities are going ahead with e-government access, their information is then not always linked to the national registries. Nada Ivankovic, a Valjevo official in the department that handles births, deaths, and marriage certificates, said these records are digitalized in her office. Such registries, however, are not interconnected with other municipalities or a central database, thereby making the access to information from other regions difficult.

»Unlike the state lottery company, which uses a single database for any ticket payment and instantly gets all the necessary data, public and state administrations have a number of separate databases,« explained Predrag Martinovic, chief of informatics and development in the Valjevo municipality.

Even where progress has been made, it has often been limited. Slobodan Markovic, spokesman of the non-profit Center for Internet Development, said there is a long way to go before Serbians will be able to submit tax forms online, or make electronic payments, mainly because the country is behind on enacting regulations on electronic signatures and privacy.

The European Commission said that Serbia needs to do more to bring its laws on personal data and privacy up to European standards. Telecommunications Minister Smiljanic said the government was currently working on a legal framework that will regulate the sharing of electronic information, such as personal and financial data.

Some Serbians think that their government needs more than just computers and technology to improve its services. Dusko Davidovic, 34, an engineer who lived in Sweden for two years, recently returned to Serbia. He described the Swedish administration as efficient, and providing most government services on the Internet.

But he believes that new technological solutions alone would not change the situation in Serbia. There needs to be a general improvement in public service. »The Swedish administration is never satisfied by its work and looks for the ways to improve it, while in our case they seem to be quite pleased with how everything is functioning,« Davidovic said.

***Larisa Rankovic**, born in 1971, studied in Belgrade, Warsaw and Rome. Currently she is a consultant for the InterMedia Institute, Washington, a media analyst in Ebart Consulting, and a journalist and contributor for Transitions Online, Netnovinar, Vreme, Republika, Danas and Ekonomist. She also writes the Media Mix blog (http://mediaserbia.blogspot.com).*

Identitet weekly magazine, Croatia, 1 June 2007

More Hatred, Less Love (2007)

By Boris Rašeta

To me and to her, Europe seems to be a good, new homeland – it is not small, it shouldn't be narrow-minded, and it should offer a good, broad framework for our lives, or even better, for our children's lives. However, the Frenchwoman and I think differently about one thing. She believes in a united, new nation.

I believe that my experience can speak against that attitude. Moreover, I really think such an attitude is very dangerous.

The Bridges of Madison County

Honestly, I didn't believe I would see Alain Delon and Mireille Darc in *The Bridges of Madison County*. One of the last performances of the play, which has been the ultimate box-office hit of the French capital since the beginning of 2007, was on Saturday, May 12, at Theatre Marigny.

On Thursday I booked the airplane ticket to Paris. There was no one answering the phone at the Marigny but on their website they said that there were still some tickets available. On Friday I had the airplane ticket in my pocket but the show was sold out, or at least it said so on the website. What bad luck!

»Ok,« I thought to myself, »I'll go to Paris anyway and spend the whole day sitting on the fourth and fifth floor of the Orsay Museum, where there is Kandinsky, Chagal and Picasso and where there is Jackson, Pollock and Basquiat. That's not bad either.«

Still, I wanted to see Delon performing live.

I had seen him play *Zorro*, then *Roco Sifreddi* in *Borsalino*, and *the samurai* in the legendary Melville's crime movie. He was the hero of my young days. Like Tito, Kusturica, Belmondo, or Goran Bregović, nicknamed Gypsy, he is an old-fashioned hero who belongs to a world that is slowly but surely disappearing.

So, this might be the last chance. Chagall will be hanging at the Orsay forever but Delon, who has performed in theatres only four times in his life and who is now 72, will surely not be treading the boards again so soon.

On Saturday morning I boarded the plane and arrived in Paris at about ten. At half past eleven I first went to Theatre Marigny. Just in case someone might return a ticket.

I was the first one there. The box office was supposed to open at eleven but there was still no one in. With the tickets being sold out, I did not even expect anyone, but suddenly a blonde woman came around the corner.

I thought she was French. She too had no ticket, but wanted to see the ex-spouses Delon and Darc play the roles which resembled their own lives in so many respects.

The wider framework is a better solution

We start to talk in poor but mutually comprehensible English. She is convinced there are still some tickets left and we just have to wait for the box office to open. While talking to each other, we begin to realize that we have something in common.

She is actually a French-German sculptor who chose France for her homeland and now hopes for a Europe in which the differences will vanish and the discomfort of national identities will be wiped out.

I am a Serb living in Croatia, and together, my French friend and I are waiting for Europe.

Both she and I feel a certain anxiety while among people of our former nations. Therefore, we believe that the wider framework is a better solution. We understand each other well. I personally do not even believe in the nation that stands for the community of trust, solidarity and values. Not any more. Actually, the only community I still believe in is the family. But even it, the family, is being more and more shaken by the challenges of our times.

She does not speak of Germany gladly, but of France much more easily, and of Europe most enthusiastically by far. She hopes her children will be Europeans. I hope so, too.

To me and to her, Europe seems to be a good, new homeland – it is not small, it shouldn't be narrow-minded, and it should offer a good, broad framework for our lives, or even better, for our children's lives. However, the Frenchwoman and I think differently about one thing. She believes in a united, new nation.

I believe that my experience can speak against that attitude. Moreover, I really think such an attitude is very dangerous.

In 1989 the Yugoslav nations were practically one step away from being melted into one.

Since Tito's death at the beginning of the '80s, the number of Serbs and Croats who declared themselves Yugoslavs had been increasing very rapidly. At the end of the decade, the Yugoslavs were enjoying considerable economic prosperity.

And then, as the book *The Old Regime and the Revolution* by Alexis de Tocqueville says, *»They did not start to fall apart at the point of hitting the bottom but at the point when they were headed upwards.«*

The identity of the new Yugoslav nation made its leading nations, the old-fashioned Serbs, Croats and Slovenes, furious as it grew ever stronger. They were by all means demographically threatened by the processes of depopulation. Consequently, Yugoslavia was crushed down and bathed in blood by the consensus of its leading nations.

That's the same danger Europe could face if it becomes deluded that there is a possibility of creating a new nation. The resistance would be terrible and at a certain point maybe even fatal.

One by one, mostly older people were slowly approaching Theatre Marigny and the concentration of the gendarmerie was becoming more and more obvious.

»You should know,« I say to her, »that Yugoslavia was built from the top twice, from the roof instead from the foundation. It was imposed and unwanted, although the idea itself sounded more than good: a micro-Europe consisting of similar but not large nations who share a similar but not old history and similar languages, and who struggle for emancipation.«

»Together we are stronger.« But that was an idea shared only by the elite groups. The first time it was imposed from the neighborhood, from Versailles, and the second time, from Moscow and London. Both times it failed ingloriously. It generated great hatred within the old nations, who saw it as a danger for their own identity. And by destroying that immediate danger, on the one hand, and longing for the national state on the other, they destroyed everything that was good about the idea itself.

»You hate each other even more and the story is over.« She knew the conclusion and shrugged her shoulders with a melancholic expression on her face.

»No,« I succeeded in surprising her. It's the other way around. The Catholics and the Protestants in Ireland hate each other a great deal more than the Serbs and Croats do. Not to mention the Arabs and the Jews. They hate each other constantly, profoundly and reliably.

In fact, somehow, we hate each other less now. If there is a difference between the Balkans and Europe, it would be these cycles of ecstatic love and hate. Within Europe there is profound hatred and no great love. We, on the other hand, hate each other for a while and afterwards, we love each other again. Now, we are connecting again. But this time the process of connection is starting at the bottom and not at the top. In their new states they all have the feeling of being their own boss now, but they grew so poor that there is nothing left to rule over. When we were rich, we were arrogant. Now when we are poor, we are being rational.

»We destroyed Marx,« I go on, »and thus proved the accuracy of Marxism.«

»Sorry, how do you mean that?«

»It's like this. According to Marx's communist recipe, the socialist community of nations and the communist economy – which were built from the top – fell apart like the castles in the air, and the capitalist economy and the liberal economic community which were built after Marx – contrary to his beliefs – seem to be of vital importance.

In his *Communist Manifesto*, Marx says that the bourgeois keeps pulling down all the frontiers in its path, including even the toughest ones, namely the national ones. This is exactly what has been happening to us. We destroyed Marx and by doing so, we in part proved him right.

After the war, the Croats and the Serbs – and they are the key factor for stability in the Balkans, by the way – organized a basketball league on their own initiative, and are going to do the same with the soccer league now. At the same time, the industry is being re-connected, money is being made, trade is expanding, advertisements go in both directions, the mass public that does not exist in the new and small countries is emerging.

»Do you see what happens during the Eurovision Song Contests?«

The Croats, Serbs, Bosnians and Slovenes, who were killing each other so wholeheartedly during the war, give each other the maximum number of points and compete with each other in the practice of tolerance and protection of the minorities.

»What do you mean by that?« she asked.

»This,« I said. »That is the repulsive paradox of tolerance. After you destroy or exile an ethnic minority – and everyone did that in the Balkans, which explains why this territory is now mostly homogenous in ethnic terms – that minority is no longer a bother, and you see it as riches and not a danger, or the corrosion on the national metal. You take care of it, pamper it ... you even start to brag about it, give recipes to others, you show off. And all that makes your own nation look progressive somehow.«

The police cars were still humming around us, and we were surrounded by more and more gendarmes whose »outfit« was awe-inspiring; they were calm, but seemed ready to fight.

A Yugoslav slogan came to my mind:

We should work as if the peace will last for 100 years, but be prepared for the war to break out tomorrow.

The formula was witty and smart, but it did not help us.

Slowly, the police officers were accumulating around the theatre.

»The gendarmerie keeps gathering here. What is going on?« I asked her.

»There is nothing going on. You see the green surface across the street?«

»Yes.«

»That is Élysée Palace there. In about ten days

Sarkozy is moving in and the gendarmerie is here only as the measure of prevention, for removing any possible obstacles. The left and the ethnic minorities hate him. Any simple reason would be sufficient to bring a repeat of the Saint Denise riots.«

»Their hatred makes sense,« I replied. »It's logical they hate him. Seen from a long-term point of view, it's logical, but not entirely wise. Instead of the constitution, Sarkozy wants an agreement defining the minimum of the common functions of the Union. He justifies the differences that cannot be eliminated. I believe he has good intentions about everything. Together with Angela Merkel, he is searching for an adequate framework for the sustainable common content. Having seen what Yugoslavia experienced, Sarkozy wants to build a building that can resist the earthquakes and wants to start building it from the bottom. That is what the Powerfrau Merkel is doing. All this may not sound great, but based on our experience, it is a better solution. It's better to have that than something else that looks like an ideal community today and would explode tomorrow!«

And, as Lenin would say: Better Less But Better!«

Sorry, I am not a Marxist,

but I do come from the cultural environment in which the quotations of the classics of Marxism-Leninism are as generally known as the slogan about equality, liberty and fraternity is in your country. We had a slogan on fraternity and unity, the slogan about an idyllic and non-conflicting community of nations. That idyllic picture was kept alive with the help of the dictatorial regime, because no one was allowed to say anything that would spoil it. You would end up in prison if you said anything against fraternity and unity. And that created the effect of a pressure cooker instead of a melting pot. In public people loved each other, but the hatred was pent up in secret. And when it exploded, there was a bang! The Balkans: a veritable powder keg.

»That is why,« I say to her, »it is good for you to have Sarkozy who discloses all this hatred publicly and controls it by deploying the gendarmerie. And thus, you should trust our experience, he is reducing the danger of explosion. The suppressed collective trauma is a potential political atomic bomb. That's how he keeps everything under control.«

The best philosopher of our region, the Slovene Slavoj Žižek, says in a nice, smart and unpopular way:

»More hatred, less love....«

By saying this he, of course, does not encourage absurd hatred but stimulates sustainable love – or, at least, tolerance, which is really better.

»Dear God, it is all about paradoxes in your world,« she said.

»You should keep these paradoxes in mind. They do not belong exclusively to us, to the Balkans, they are the European experience. Just look at our war camps from the end of the century. They resemble the German ones a lot, which happened earlier in time but surpassed them in perfection. Only this can be referred to as the differentia specifica of the Balkans. We are an eminent Europe, but also Europe which is a bit more at ease, Europe using some other means, Europe which has a little bit more blood on its hands, but we are Europe in any case.«

It would be dangerous if Europe weren't to realize that.

The box office opened at about half past eleven. Both my collocutor and I got tickets for *The Bridges of Madison County.* In the play we saw the two European stars who were the stars before the Europe of today. In times when today's EU was just a weak community for coal and steel, its cultural sphere was domineered by Antonioni, Visconti, Delon, Belmondo, Brandauer, Fassbinder, Godard....

Today, Europe is a political community and its common cultural grounds are even weaker than those of the old community for coal and steel. There are no more European stars.

Young Croats may have heard of Gérard Depardieu or Juliette Binoche, but no one has ever heard of Daniel Autieul or Ulrich Muech. In France everyone knows Emir Kusturica, but no one knows Dušan Kovačević. None of the German and Czech actors are known in Croatia.

From Bergman onwards, the Croats are not familiar with the Scandinavian films; maybe some younger people are familiar with the work of Aki Kaurismaki. That's sad.

Maybe then, we will talk again

All these are the paradoxes I did not have time to discuss with my unexpected acquaintance. We bought the tickets and went our own ways.

In a year or so, both she and I will be living within the same frontiers. Maybe then, we will talk again.

As to the paradoxes we talked about, we do not have the solutions anyway.

We can only keep our eyes open and try not to get killed by the scary potential of the content, which we, the people from the Balkans, are not going to underestimate ever again.

***Boris Rašeta** was born 1968 in Bihać (Bosnia and Herzegovina). He studied sociology at the University of Zagreb. He has written for various media since 1991 including the television station Yutel, the news magazine Danas, the Croatian anti-war magazine Arkzin. He has written for Feral Tribune for ten years and for the critical television programme Latinica for two* *years. During the Yugoslav wars, he was a Croatian correspondent for the Belgrade weekly newspaper Vreme, and was an editor at the Bosnian office of the German radio station Deutsche Welle for many years. Rašeta also works for the weekly magazine Identitet of the Serbian Democratic Forum in Zagreb. Since 2005, he has also been a Croatian correspondent for the German press agency Deutsche Presse Agentur and editor of the Croatian newspaper 24 sata.*

Glasove weekly, Bulgaria, November 2007

Bulgarians are the Greatest Evil of Bulgaria, Mister! (2008)

By Vlado Trifonov

Dusseldorf Airport. I am calmly waiting for the airplane to Gothenburg, closely studying the people around me.

One with the face of an office accountant simultaneously moves his fingers and lips. A man and a woman holding hands jabber; more precisely, she talks all the time and he agrees to everything she says by nodding and smiling. A man advanced in years, is discreetly flirting on his cell phone. Another one reads a book, carefully thumbing the pages and, how unique! – does not lick his finger to get a better grip.

Everything is clean and quiet. There is nothing extraordinary to catch my attention, and I begin to feel very drowsy. That is, until an elegant, well-dressed elderly lady with black high-heeled shoes shows up, wearing a coquettish cap, a stylish shoulder bag, and modern, long earrings. Her quick movements, her upright posture, and her vitality stand in total contrast to the rather bleak, unpretentious airport hall. Luxury, elegance and energy electrify the air.

Information regarding our delayed flight, due to bad weather, is spreading. The old lady takes a look at her watch, and then sits down on an empty seat close to me, with a view towards the airstrips. She takes a quick look at the people in the hall and then digs into her handbag and pulls out a crumpled Bulgarian newspaper. She checks it in a hurry; holds it for a moment at some page, saying »my God«, and reads on.

Suddenly I hear my own voice:

»I used to write for that newspaper some time ago«.

»Ah, so-o-o! But are you Bulgarian?« – the old lady reacts as quick as lightning. Then she looks at the newspaper disdainfully - »Communist! Here I have another one,« she says, and pulls out a second Bulgarian newspaper. »It is also communist. In Bulgaria they only sell communist newspapers«.

»I used to write for that one as well. I had a column about decent Bulgarians.« »

»Ah, so-o-o! But are you also...?«

»No, I'm not. This time I was faster than she«

Soon we are immersed in a conversation. The old lady is pleased, because I am giving her my full attention and listening patiently. I am also satisfied, because she is such an unusual person, the sort of person I haven't come across for a long time.

»You say you've been writing about decent Bulgarians. But where did you find any decent Bulgarians? Cheats, burglars and criminals - that what today's Bulgarians are, mister. And they all are communists. Seems like there are no other people in Bulgaria except Gypsies and communists. And those who pretend not to be communists later prove to be the biggest ones. But now they are all turning into capitalists.

»Capitalists and bodyguards. But I don't want to mix things up. Bodyguards they were! And whose body did they guard? They are cowards, not bodyguards. I talked to one of them in Bulgaria and asked him – ›Do you want to hit me? Do you want to fight with me, you coward? With an old woman? Why don't you fight Holyfield? Why don't you beat Schwarzenegger up? Because they would all smash you up, that's why.‹

»Bulgarians are the true problem of Bulgaria, mister! Not Gypsies, not Turks. I apologize for what I am saying, and I say all of this with sorrow, because I am Bulgarian. Evenif I ldid leave Bulgaria many years ago. Bulgarians are the greatest enemy of this beautiful country. I dream of it, and I will dream of it until I die. Do you know how old I am? I am 80. But if I would have stayed in Bulgaria I would no longer be alive. I would have died of anger, mister.

»I don't try to keep in touch with Bulgarians. I have other friends - all kinds, but no Bulgarians! Because even abroad, Bulgarians remain Bulgarians – their envy eats them up. They are eaten up by envy, greed and by ignorance, mister. Almost all of the plump, fat communists live in foreign countries. Just like their money, which they placed in Swiss, English, and American banks. They stole the money in Bulgaria and then they left the country to spend what they stole.

»Who stayed in Bulgaria? The small fishes stayed. Bulgaria suits them, because there are still some pieces of the cake left for them. It seems as if this Bulgarian pastry is very tasty, mister, tasty and cheap.

»I was in Bansko, a town which has been cut to pieces and swallowed. I went to visit the Black Sea – everything is gone. Rila Mountain, Pirin Mountain – those old communist party gangsters will destroy everything. They and their sons, daughters, grandsons and bodyguards. They should all be sentenced and sent to prison, just like all politicians – down to the very last one! They demoralized the nation. They forced people to be like them – greedy and corrupt.

»My father was a factory owner. He played the piano and spoke five languages. He always said to me: ›the greedier a nation, the easier it is to govern.‹ That's what Bulgaria is now. They have made the Bulgarians miserable, emotionally dissatisfied, and bad-looking creatures. Thievish and dishonest, with no dignity.

»Don't I have anything nice to say? Nice like what, mister? Like that Minister of Emergency who bought 40 cars for her office? By God – 40 cars!

Who paid for so many cars? Drag her out of her Mercedes, giving her a kick in her behind, sit her on a mule's back and take her straight to prison – that's what she deserves.

»Jail is the right place for her – for her and for all the other ministers who ruined this country. This is what I call a conspiracy, mister. Who gets rich in Bulgaria these days? The bandits get rich. The drug dealers get rich. All those nasty looking communists – they get rich. Even if you want to earn clean money, you can't; they hinder all your efforts. They will force you to be like them. Otherwise – a bullet is waiting for you.

»How can one fight them? I don't know, and that's why I fled. You only fight against something if you have at least a small chance of succeeding. But not against organized and heavily armed criminals: those on the street and those in parliament.

»The West? The West needs a good punch. I am a German-, English- and French-speaking person, mister. The same thing is written in all the newspapers I read: the communists are the ones who pull all the strings in Bulgaria. But nobody asks where all the money went. Is their money on Western bank accounts? Sure. But how can their money be accepted there, if everybody – even a dog – knows that this money was stolen? Let me tell you how: the West doesn't give a damn whether that money is stolen or not, mister. The most important thing is that it is money and it flows into Western accounts.

»Let me ask you about your decent Bulgarians. What did they do? Did they spark off a revolution and kick the communists out – far away and forever? They didn't. And they will never do so. Bulgarians don't need democracy. They don't know what to do with democracy. What Bulgarians need is a master, and then they feel good. They need a master who gives orders and who can subdue the Bulgarian people.. Bulgarians can't become Europeans. That's impossible. The Bulgarian soul is different, its nature is different. Europe? Europe wants Bulgaria's money and Bulgaria's market, but not the Bulgarian people.

»What about the intellectuals? You can't simply be an intellectual. First, you must be noble. You must have a free spirit and a sense of elegance. Intellect has never been a quality of the masses, but Bulgaria is a place for the masses, mister. A mass infected by communism. The intellectuals in this country have always ended up badly. Most of them died – some of them abroad, others in camps.

»My friend Dora Valie died in Paris. She was a real intellectual. May her memory live forever. Her brother, Petar Uvaliev, died in London. He was an intellectual, and God forgive him. These kinds of people no longer exist. Today, you only have those who pretend to be intellectuals and they are appointed as such. They were told: ›From today on, we appoint you an intellectual.‹

»And the youngsters? The youngsters will not be able to make things any better. They resemble the ones they live with. The youngsters imitate what they see. When they see greed and criminality all about them, what do you expect from them – that they become democrats? No mister, all they could do is become emigrants.«

...

They call the passengers for the flight to Gothenburg. I look at my watch – we have been delayed by about one hour. One hour spent in conversation with a Bulgarian woman who has been living abroad for almost half a century. A Bulgarian woman for whom Bulgaria still is an open wound, and most likely will remain so forever.

»If you want to write about me, please write that an old lady said: ›The Bulgarians are the greatest evil of Bulgaria.‹

»It was my pleasure, mister.«

***Vlado Trifonov**, Bulgarian freelance journalist and documentary filmmaker. Graduated from Charles University in Prague, Czech Republic, Film & Theater Sciences. He specializes in mass media and scriptwriting. Trifonov writes film, theater and TV reviews; he* *is a publicist and scriptwriter. As a journalist Vlado Trifonov sometimes writes under the pseudonym Victor Ankov.*